TESTIMONIALS

This is an inspirational must-read as we all question *what is our why?* Patience has walked the journey in her STEM career and has shared with us what true grit to succeed against all odds means in the male dominated work environment of mining. She shares a deep passion for empowering women and closing the gender gap, and is making a huge contribution to a critical SDG. This book is a highly commendable read on gender equality, especially in male-dominated STEM related industries like mining. It is indeed a call to action.

—Professor Shirley Zinn, Independent Non-Executive Director on the Boards of JSE-listed companies and Executive Director at the Boston Consulting Group SA. South Africa

Patience's incredible story of her journey to recognition of her superpowers is an inspiration for all women and girls and not only those in STEM. With grit, determination, overcoming setbacks and taking risks, she succeeded in the male dominated mining industry and now shares her wisdom to help other women succeed. *Unleashing My Superpowers* is indeed a must-read book for every woman striving to succeed.

—Clare Beckton, Fulbright Scholar, Littauer fellow Harvard, Author of *OWN-IT Your Success, your Future, Your Life*. Canada

Unleashing My Superpowers is a fascinating book that gives perspectives on resilience and passion to succeed. If you have ever felt stuck and you don't know how to navigate the complex male dominated workplace like mining then this is a must read!

—Heike Truol, Non-Executive Director Clarkson plc and former Executive Head Anglo American plc. United Kingdom

First congratulations, loved reading your book! This is a must read! Patience has captured the tools and skills we all need. When you read her book, you will identify yourself with many of her stories. Her story is captivating and brings alive what it is to live and succeed in a male dominated industry like mining. Its about perseverance and unleashing your superpowers that ultimately makes you succeed.

—Anna Tudela, Board Member, Canadian Centre for Diversity and Inclusion and Former Vice President for Gold Corp Resources. Canada.

An impressive book about an exceptional woman that provides women with insights into how they can manage the difficult challenges of a woman building a career and working in the male dominated STEM oriented workplace of the mining industry. *Unleashing My Superpowers* provides insights that are not only invaluable to women, but also to men, in how to support female colleagues and make change that will enhance the mining industry and also other industries and make them better places to work and succeed for all.

—Professor Barbara Messerle, former Executive Dean, Faculty of Science and Engineering, Macquarie University, Former Deputy-Vice Chancellor of the University of Sydney, and visiting Professor at UNSW. Australia.

Patience uses her superpower of storytelling to provide an inspirational but practical guide for all of us striving for Peak Performance! I know first-hand that she not only preaches and teaches the lessons she shares, she truly lives them. I am grateful for Patience, this project and book, and thrilled that so many will be touched and empowered by Patience and this extraordinary work.

—Shannon O. Pierce, IWF Fellow Alumni and 20-year Energy Executive. USA

Dr. Patience Mpofu is a woman of great courage, resilience, and inspiration. Congratulations! This book is inspirational for those who wish to crash through the glass ceiling in a male-dominated world of STEM and mining. Patience shares a compelling story of how she navigated the tough mining industry to become well known as a Global Thought Leader in ESG and thus winning several awards in the mining industry in Africa. Her story proves that anything is possible when we stand on the shoulders of moral giants, believe in ourselves, and wish to serve the greater good.

—Anne Pratt, Harvard fellow, multi-awarded businesswoman, upcoming author *Mandela's Leadership Blueprint*. South Africa.

Practical and inspiring! A combination of her personal story and examples, Patience has turned her trailblazing career in the mining and metals industry into supporting and paving the way for other women in STEM coming up against the same barriers she experienced on her way to success across the globe. A must read for every woman in STEM, and males in the mining industry!

—Helena De Oliviera, IWF Fellow Alumni and Executive Transformational Leader. Canada

Unleashing My Superpowers is a wonderful reflection of Patience's authenticity, resilience and her passion to pay it forward. I met Patience as an IWF Fellow and her story connected with my heart when I first heard her speak. Her warmth and passion radiate through this wonderfully inspiring must-read.

—Kate Nuttall, IWF Fellow Alumni and Human Resources Leader. Australia

Unleashing My Superpowers is an important must-read leadership book for the 21st Century. In this inspiring book, Dr Patience Mpofu shares her own personal story of overcoming adversity and rising above life's challenges to become Africa's most influential woman in mining. Patience uses these life lessons to help guide and pave the way for others by creating a blueprint for women in STEM professions and leadership globally. She provides practical exercises for individuals to identify and express their own unique superpowers and invites organisations to cultivate environments that advance greater diversity, equity and inclusion for everyone.

—Hayley Moffiet-Wong, Founder of Architects of Change Network. Australia

UNLEASHING MY SUPERPOWERS

How to Navigate and Succeed in a Male-Dominated Mining Work Environment (STEM)

Dr Patience Mpofu

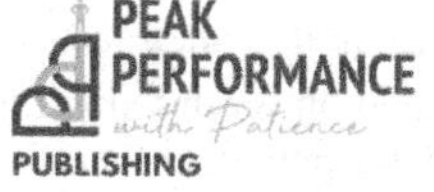

Unleashing My Superpowers

www.unleashingmysuperpowers.com

Copyright © 2021 DR PATIENCE MPOFU

ISBN 978-0-6452337-1-1 (paperback)
ISBN 978-0-6452337-2-8 (hardback)
ISBN 978-0-6452337-0-4 (e-Book)

References to internet websites (URLs) were accurate at the time of writing. The author and publishers are not responsible for URLs that may have expired or changed since the manuscript was prepared.

Limits of Liability and Disclaimer of Warranty
The author and publisher shall not be liable for your misuse of the enclosed material. This book is strictly for informational and educational purposes only.

Warning – Disclaimer
The purpose of this book is to educate and entertain. The author and/or publisher do not guarantee that anyone following these techniques, suggestions, tips, ideas, or strategies will become successful. The author and/or publisher shall have neither liability nor responsibility to anyone with respect to any loss or damage caused, or alleged to be caused, directly or indirectly by the information contained in this book.

Medical Disclaimer
The medical or health information in this book is provided as an information resource only, and is not to be used or relied on for any diagnostic or treatment purposes. This information is not intended to be patient education, does not create any patient-physician relationship, and should not be used as a substitute for professional diagnosis and treatment.

Peak Performance with Patience Publisher Sydney, Australia. Printed worldwide including Australia, United States of America, Canada, United Kingdom, South Africa etc

TABLE OF CONTENTS

I dedicate this book to my mother for her strength, compassion and sacrifices as my role model, to my father for his belief in me, and to my son for his unconditional love and solidarity.

LIST OF FREQUENTLY USED ABBREVIATIONS

AMP	Advanced Management Programme
BEE	Black Economic Empowerment
C-Suite	Executive-level managers within a company
DMRE	Department of Minerals and Resources Energy
ESG	Environment, Social and Governance
Exco	Executive Committee
GCE O & A	General Certificate of Education, Ordinary and Advanced Levels
GICC	Global Innovation Coalition for Change
HDSA	Historically Disadvantaged South Africans
HR	Human Resources
IDC	Industrial Development Corporation
IWF	International Women's Forum
IWRI	Ian Wark Research Institute
KPI	Key Performance Indicators
LGBTQIA	Lesbian, Gay, Bisexual, Pansexual, Transgender, Queer, Intersex, Agender, Asexual
MDP	Management Development Programme
M&A	Mergers and Acquisitions
NGO	Non-Governmental Organisation
NUST	National University of Science and Technology
NLP	Neuro-Linguistic Programming
SA	South Africa
SDGs	Sustainable Development Goals
STEM	Science, Technology, Engineering and Mathematics
UN	United Nations

UNDP	United Nations Development Programme
UNFPA	United Nations Population Fund
UNICEF	United Nations Children's Fund
UNISA	University of South Australia
UNW	United Nations Women
VP	Vice President
WBS	Witwatersrand Business School

Peak Performance Executive Coaching:
Unleashing Your Superpowers

Executive Leadership: We help you unleash your superpowers.

Are you a woman in STEM, feeling stuck and wondering: *How do I navigate to succeed in a male dominated workplace such as mining?*

Did you know? From a survey we conducted across the globe of women in C-Suite in male dominated workplaces (STEM):

98% said: *If we have more women in leadership positions, more women will succeed.*

70% believe: *the biggest barrier in getting more women promoted is that there are no women in senior positions.*

98% believe: *when women support each other, more women will succeed.*

More than 81% said: *having a coach and mentor helped them with navigating the work environment and acting as a sounding board.*

84% said: *having the right quality of network and belonging to a group of likeminded people has helped them to break the glass ceiling for their careers.*

You don't have to feel alone. Join our community and follow us on our social media platforms for free resources to unleash your superpowers to succeed:

Facebook
https://www.facebook.com/groups/peakperformancewithpatience

LinkedIn
https://www.linkedin.com/company/peakperformancewithpatience

Instagram
https://www.instagram.com/drpatiencempofu_stemcoach/

Twitter
@DrPatienceMpofu

YouTube
http://bit.ly/UnleashingMySuperpowers

Coaching may increase your chances of success.

Subscribe and join our Unleashing My Superpowers academy to claim your free bonuses immediately by scanning the QR code here:

ABOUT THE AUTHOR

Dr. Patience Mpofu is a multi-award-winning mining executive, International Women's Forum 2018 Fellow, Global Thought Leader in sustainability and Environmental, Social and Governance (ESG), Executive Leadership Coach, and Women in STEM advocate.

A Zimbabwean born, South African citizen, Patience has turned her trailblazing career in the mining and metals industry into empowering and paving the way for other women coming up against the same barriers she experienced on her way to success across the globe.

After earning her PhD in mineral processing at the University of South Australia, and a string of high-profile senior executive leadership roles with mining company giants in South Africa and Australia, she was recognised as one of the 36 women leaders from around the world to take part in the prestigious 2018–2019 International Women's Forum Fellows Program, an honour that changed the course of her path.

Patience has turned these challenges into grit and ambition, propelling her career from lead metallurgist to senior roles across disciplines. She is an accomplished sustainable development strategist with more than 25 years' experience working in the mining and metals industry. Prior to founding her businesses, she was Vice President Corporate Affairs Africa of a global Australian mining company. Using her experiences and relationships in these high-level roles, she works towards closing gender gaps in the hope of achieving the United Nations for Sustainable Development Agenda goal 5 by 2030.

In 2017, Patience was invited by the United Nations Under Secretary General and Executive Director of UN Women to be a member of the UN Women Global Innovation and Coalition for

Change (GICC) (2017–2019), focused on accelerating and removing barriers to the advancement of women and girls in STEM. In 2019, Patience was the winner of both the CEO Most Influential Woman in Mining in Business and Government in South Africa and southern Africa. In 2020, she was again awarded the CEO Global Most Influential Woman in Government and Business in the mining sector for Africa. Patience has spoken at key global events such as the Mining Indaba, where she launched the first Women in Mining luncheon in 2017, attracting industry influencers and keynote speakers including the Minister for Women in the Presidency and Senator for Western Australia. She was also a panellist at this luncheon, discussing challenges of diversity and inclusion in mining. She is passionate about diversity, equity and inclusion in the mining industry and helping women navigate the often-complex mining work environment to advance in their professions.

Patience now spends her days as a sustainable development mining expert, helping to advance critical sustainable development goals for mining companies, ensuring they meet ESG metrics, and as an executive leadership coach for women in STEM. Her mining experiences have sparked a love for using her trials and tribulations to help other women have the same opportunities as their male counterparts. She uses her voice as a global sought-after speaker to get more women and, more so, male champions to help women in STEM unleash their superpowers. As part of her IWF Fellows Program Legacy Project, she successfully launched a 100-day campaign that attracted over 30 successful women in STEM and interviewed them on what it takes to succeed in a male-dominated work environment. The inspirational women included an astronaut who spent over 180 days in space and a global leader who met Mandela. This book is part of her IWF Fellows Program Legacy Project.

Patience is the founder and CEO of Peak Performance Executive Leadership Coaching. She is also a director and partner of the mining consulting firm Insight Mining Experts, a global platform that connects technology experts to help solve sustainability issues in the mining industry and help them meet their ESG commitments.

Patience holds an Advanced Management Program from INSEAD and an MBA from Wits Business School. She has published over 10 peer-reviewed international papers and presentations on sustainability in reducing water consumption in the mining industry.

She is the mother of a son, William, who is her pillar of strength, and she is close to her family. She currently lives between Sydney, Australia and Johannesburg, South Africa.

> *The meaning of life is to find your gift;*
> *the purpose of life is to give it away.*
> — William Shakespeare

You can follow or reach her via:

Email: info@peakperformancewithpatience.com
Instagram: @drpatiencempofu_stemcoach
Twitter: @DrPatienceMpofu
Facebook: Dr Patience Mpofu
LinkedIn: https://www.linkedin.com/in/drpatiencempofu/
Website: www.unleashingmysuperpowers.com and www.peakperformancewithpatience.com

ACKNOWLEDGEMENTS

I acknowledge many people who have helped me realise my dream to write and publish this book. First and foremost, my son, William Nkanyiso Mpofu, is my advisor. He is dedicated, supportive and fun. His being there for me and encouraging me in the midst of the COVID-19 pandemic was surreal. I was feeling depleted towards the last chapters, but he said, 'Keep going Mum'. My pillar of strength. Thank you.

To my humble mother, Parto Mawarire Nhongo, an African woman, for being the greatest role model as a compassionate and strong woman. She sacrificed everything to raise and educate all of her seven kids, putting others first and not leaving anyone behind, through her relentless efforts to make a difference in other people's lives. She is my champion. I am thankful for the values she instilled, to think of others and be a compassionate leader. You are my hero.

My late father, Stephen Nhongo, a man who believed that a girl or woman can be anything she wants to be, without limitations. I underestimated the influence you had on us as girls. If you had listened to the old traditions of not educating girls, if you had not prioritised our education, if you had not taught us that there is no male or female job—I wouldn't be where I am today. Even though I hated checking the car for oil leaks, and the water tank, and changing tyres, I now understand why you did that. Thank you for telling us to use our heads, and thank you for forcing us to use our brains instead of a calculator. You truly stretched us to be the best version of ourselves and to unleash our superpowers. *I am because of you.* I know you are smiling in your grave and thinking, *these are my girls.* It is sad that you have not been able to enjoy the fruits of your labour and see your grandchildren.

Many thanks to my family for their unwavering support and assistance, especially my sisters and brother for constantly phoning just to get me motivated. Peddie, Pepsi, Fadzai, Diana, Zodwa, Tinashe, Zanele, Theo, Tracy and Faith. The boundless support of my family has been the foundation of my life. My uncle, Simon Nhongo, really helped me write and review my chapter on the history of the Lemba.

I gratefully acknowledge the IWF for giving me an opportunity to participate in the prestigious Fellows Program that inspired me to write this book as part of my legacy project to help close the gender gap. I wouldn't have had the courage and motivation to undertake this project otherwise. Many thanks to Jessa Cooke, the late Dr. Vuyo Mahlati, and Catherine Curry-Hyde for helping me get the Legacy Project off the ground. Many thanks to my mentor, Clare Beckton, for encouraging me and motivating me to keep going, despite the challenges I faced. COVID-19 almost made me give up, as I thought no one would be interested in reading my book, as everyone was facing the devastating effects of the pandemic.

I acknowledge the support of the 30 female leaders who participated in interviews. Not only did they provide me with insight into my own leadership journey, but they also added an amazing body of knowledge about what it takes for women to succeed in a male-dominated work environment. Many thanks to the IWF Fellows 2018–2019 sisters for their support, especially the ones who helped me with this project, participated in the interviews, or reviewed my manuscript: Helena De Oliviera, Nadeen Matthews, Sonar Thekdi, Samantha Zhu, Martha Herrera Gonzalez, Kate Nuttall and Shannon Pierce. I thank the amazing team that volunteered and helped me with the survey and social media: Diana Zhou, Millicent Molete and the 100 women who participated in the survey. I am blessed to be surrounded by a tribe of amazingly supportive global female leaders through this project and thank them for their wisdom in reviewing my manuscript: Professor Shirley Zinn, Heike Truol, Clare Beckton, Professor Barbara Messerle, Anna Tudela and Anne Pratt.

I greatly acknowledge my friend Hayley Wong for providing me with encouragement, checking in, and reviewing my manuscript. To my dear friend who came up with the original book design, Ninon Ocker, thank you.

It would be amiss for me not to acknowledge the many people who made my leadership journey enriching and memorable with experiences, exciting and sometimes challenging. To my two PhD Supervisors at the former IWRI, UNISA, Professor John Ralston and Professor Jonas Addai Mensah, thank you for your unwavering support throughout my PhD experience. Thank you to all my former IWRI colleagues and professors.

To the mining company Anglo American and all my former leaders and networks in that company, especially Peter Charlesworth, Sandy Lambert, Paul Dempsey, Mike Rogers, Pat Lowry, Wilm Ser, Dr Gordon Smith, Archie Myezwa, Silas Mokoele, Anthea Bath, Anthony Anyimadu, Dr Bolha, Fortune Mashimbye, Matome Leseilane, Buang Moloto, Zandile Fuyane, Heike Truol, July Ndlovu, Lloyd Nelson, Killian Manyuchi, Deshnee Naidoo, Thelma Kale, Livhu Magidimisa, Les Bryson and many others. You nurtured me to grow in many roles and provided an environment that was equal, with opportunities for all, regardless of colour, gender or creed. To the "girls club" in planning, Lana Van Wyk and my dearest friend Bon Mathibe. Thank you, Bon, for being the greatest ally throughout my career.

To my former leaders and colleagues at other companies, Cindy Mogotsi and the former Lonmin plc, I would like to acknowledge everyone, especially Lerato Molebatsi, Greg Hunter, Tanya Chikanza, Jan Geenen, Abey Kgotle, Happy Nkhoma, Natascha Viljoen, Wilma Swart, Ruli Diseko, Welcome Ndlovu, Sibongile Solombela, Mark Munroe and Ben Magara.

I am indebted to the leaders who have given me opportunities and support during my career at South32. To Mike Fraser and Ron Langford, you believed in me and gave me an opportunity to join South32, to be led and to lead. To all my former colleagues, especially Danie Murray and Lucas Msimanga. When I faced struggles, you remained consistent in supporting me. To my former leader, Kelly O'Rourke, thank you for the short time we spent together. To Katie Tovich, thank you for supporting my quest to further develop myself through IWF. To Retsibile Masondo, Nellie Okuthe and your HR team, thanks for supporting me and my team and continuing to be the best in HR. To my former team members, the entire 32 corporate affairs team, thank you for igniting a passion I never knew existed in sustainability. You made my coming to work worthwhile and exciting. There's never a dull moment leading the South African Corporate Affairs Team!

To Raymond Aaron, a truly inspiring leader and international best-selling author, and his team, who served as the main editors, managing the publication process with great skill and enthusiasm and passion for this project. Thank you for pushing me to ensure I get this book done despite taking so long.

To all my mentors, coaches and advisors and male champions who have made my journey memorable. To Tony Robbins, you are truly an inspirational global leader who changes people's lives. Thank you.

Finally, to my source, my spiritual father, God Almighty, for always being there with me. Even as I walked in the valley of darkness, I feared nothing. Thank you.

This book is an appreciation of the mining industry and of its leaders who shaped my journey to becoming a global leader and a force for good. Thank you.

FOREWORD

Are you feeling stuck in your career or business? Are you a woman working in a STEM-related profession, or in an industry such as mining, and struggling to navigate the male dominated work environment?

Despite recent advances in trying to close the gender gap in male-dominated workplaces, there are still invisible barriers preventing you, as a woman, from succeeding in these industries. Because of ESG requirements for mining companies to close the gender gap, especially in C-Suite, I am excited to endorse this book, *Unleashing My Superpowers: How to Navigate and Succeed in a Male-Dominated Mining Work Environment.*

Dr Patience Mpofu has taken a topic that is not often discussed, and used her story to help you, as a woman in a similar situation. Through her story, she shares how your upbringing influences and shapes your career choices and your success.

Her friendly and conversational tone will win you over, and her demonstrated acumen on the global mining industry and leadership subject will excite you. You will quickly find safety in her leadership stories and practical examples, such as how she overcame her fear of imposter syndrome. She encourages you to change your story and use your voice as a force for good, to unleash your superpowers as a compassionate, courageous leader.

After reading *Unleashing My Superpowers*, you will be empowered to understand your *why*, your mission, and your purpose. You will know how to unleash your superpowers, to help you to get promoted and to succeed in your career as a leader.

Her story will inspire you to reach for your dreams, and to have the courage and confidence to speak up, to ask for what you want. *Unleashing My Superpowers* provides a one stop shop mentorship from someone who has walked the journey working in a STEM career field, and will help you to navigate the male dominated workplace, balancing your career and your personal life.

Get ready to read this amazing journey and create a massive change in your life and career. You can unleash your superpowers to succeed!

Raymond Aaron
New York Times Bestselling Author

INTRODUCTION

If not me, then who, if not now, then when?
— Rabbi Hillel

Unleashing My Superpowers, by Dr Patience Mpofu

I lost my voice but now I have found it
I am the voice
The voice that is courageous, confident
The voice that speaks the truth
The voice that unleashes love
The voice that unleashes trust
I have finally unleashed my superpowers

When your world seems dark
When the world seems to crumble
It is in the darkest of moments
That the infinite power reveals itself
To help you unleash your superpowers

And when you do, help others to
Unleash their superpowers

Why This Book?

I pondered whether I should still write this book or if I should start working on my mining consultancy business. These were the thoughts in my head as the COVID-19 pandemic ravaged the world. I struggled, sat up, paced, yawned and finally slept. As I drifted to sleep, I could hear the cry of a woman working in male-dominated (STEM) workplaces like mining: *With COVID-19 already ravaging the world, I may be a victim of retrenchments as I have been struggling to navigate my workplace. I have to prove myself and my capabilities regularly despite my experience, and work twice as hard as my male colleagues, but I still have not been promoted. I have to cope with aggression, competitiveness, and being interrupted and spoken over. How will I ever cope with managing myself, my family and forever demanding work with no help at home? How do I make this happen? I wish I had someone to discuss these challenges with, and someone to guide me through these challenges.* While those thoughts were going on in my mind, I abruptly woke up and decided: This is it. I am going ahead. I am doing this. If not me, then who? If not now, then when?

I am often asked, *what inspired you to go into a male-dominated workplace like the mining industry?* The journey of sharing my personal story started on a particular day. It was in April 2018, during the Easter holidays. I was sitting by a fireside, sipping a glass of shiraz wine during the winter season of Lesotho, a small country nestled within the South African borders on the southern side. I was quietly watching my son, nephew, two nieces, and my sisters laughing and enjoying themselves. I was at peace. I felt a sense of gratitude and contentment as I was surrounded by the people who matter the most in my life. Unfortunately, my mother could not join us then due to ill health. I was reflecting on the highs and lows of my career, and all I had was a sense of gratitude and achievement. It suddenly dawned on me that in a month's time, I would be leaving the mining industry in which I had spent more than 25 years. I reflected on when this all started: How and why did I choose this industry? How did I get to where I am today? Who was my cheerleader? Who was my sponsor? I was overwhelmed by mixed feelings. I was sad that I was leaving the industry that had been home to me for over 25 years, and the relationships I had formed with various people. I was excited about the new journey, which at that time was about self-discovery. I had bought a book, *Eat, Pray, Love,* by Gilbert (2006), to get some inspiration for this journey that I was about to embark upon.

A sense of pride swept through me as the steam from the freezing weather of the beautiful Afriski ski resort in Lesotho came out with my breath. I had never felt so cold. I was tired after our travel to Afriski. We had just registered on arrival and immediately gone straight to our first skiing lesson. My first day was not the greatest; I was not focussed and all I wanted to do was to relax and just be. I had spent the past six months on what felt like a roller coaster. I had not taken a single break and I was exhausted from the company's restructuring. I needed to get away to revive, relax and reflect. This, I knew, was what effective leaders do as I had been coached about taking care of myself. I also wanted to spend time with my mum, who was not well. She needed surgery and we were contemplating whether she should have both the operations she required, or not. While I have spent most of my life in South Africa, work has meant that I never really had enough time for my family. As I pondered, I heard my name being called by my little niece, Tamara. 'Auntie, why didn't you join us? You should have seen how amazing we were. Skiing is so much fun'. I was just happy for them and to sit and enjoy my glass of wine near the fire.

We had all flown from different countries to meet for a short holiday in Lesotho where my sister Pepsi worked for UNAIDS. It had become a tradition as we are all scattered across the world, and we made that decision to get together for a regional or international trip every two years. This time, we chose Afriski in Lesotho, a beautiful country with its lush and mountainous landscape. It has so much to offer for tourists all over the world. It is a high-altitude, landlocked kingdom encircled by South Africa, and has a network of rivers and mountain ranges, including the 3,482-metre-high peak of Thabana Ntlenyana. The capital, Maseru, has ruins dating from the 19th century reign of King Moshoeshoe I. With a population of over 2.125 million, it's a relatively small country.

We left early in the morning to avoid traffic, to enjoy the beautifully scenic drive on winding mountainous roads, and to ensure we arrived before dusk. Afriski is a popular ski resort where many Africans go to learn how to ski. It is the only skiing resort in Lesotho, located 3050 metres above sea level in the Maluti Mountains. It is one of only two ski resorts in southern Africa, a 4.5-hour drive from Johannesburg. The resort offers a variety of activities including mountain biking, paintball, and hiking, and people love the night life with music and dancing.

The kids were all tired and were sleeping on the way. I was driving with my older sister. We always took advantage of long drives to chat and catch up on her work, her business and her mentoring, as I always look to her for wisdom and help with decisions. She didn't know I was taking a long-term sabbatical and leaving the corporate world, so we discussed this at length, and she appreciated my decision. The drive was delightful, and apart from getting lost, we arrived in good time.

We had booked one big house that accommodated large families so we could all be together. It was freezing that night and there was more snow than there had been the other times we had been there. We decided to order some pizza and have our wine in the house. The chatting started. The fire downstairs was ready, and it was nice and cosy. When we get together with my family, there is always plenty of laughter, teasing and craziness. My son, nephews and nieces call it the crazy family holidays. They think we are the craziest family.

The wine was flowing, the music was fun, and all was so lovely that I didn't want it to end. I always look forward to these family holidays. It must have been past midnight and we were all tired when we said our goodnights to each other and retreated to our bedrooms. I fell asleep the moment my head hit the pillow. I dreamt I was walking along a long hallway, with lights flashing and blinding me. I couldn't breathe, and I was shouting for help. As I was having this nightmare, suddenly I couldn't breathe. I thought I was still having the dream, until I consciously knew it was real. I threw the bedsheets off my chest. I struggled to find my voice, and I was gasping for air.

I dragged myself out of bed still gasping for air. I was feeling dizzy and almost blinded as I walked through the bedroom doorway to near the bathroom entrance where I fell and collapsed to the floor. I found my voice and managed to call out, 'Sis, I can't breathe!' Everyone woke up, except my son, nephew and nieces, who were sleeping downstairs. My sisters surrounded me, shaken and flooding me with questions I couldn't answer immediately. 'What happened? Are you okay?' My sister Peddie rushed to get me some water. Pepsi called medical emergency, while Diana tried to calm me. There was commotion all around. As I gulped the water and the windows were opened, I was breathing, but with difficulty. Pepsi was still trying to get hold of emergency. I could see their fear as they thought they had almost lost me. I sat up and found I could breathe more normally again, my head was spinning and I felt a bit of a headache. We decided not to persist in trying to call emergency as I felt better. I went back to sleep but was scared that I might die in through the night. My son William, nephew Mayibongwe and two nieces, Thembelihle and Tamara, were downstairs fast asleep and never heard anything.

In the morning, I was much better, but with some light-headedness. We had our breakfast, then headed to our ski lessons where we had so much fun. We didn't speak about what happened the previous night; it was as if nothing had happened. In the evening, we were dancing as usual and teasing each other. We had a competition to see who could perform the best popular dance moves for kids. We had our cosy fireplace and so much laughter was going on. Then, as we were laughing and our children were calling us the crazy family, my sister Peddie said, 'You will miss us, the crazy family, when one day we are dead. Talking about death, Auntie Patience almost died last night'. They laughed it off as a joke, but Peddie insisted and said it was not a joke. They didn't believe it until I showed them the bump I had on my face from my fall. I also had a mark on my hand where I had scratched myself. They gave me hugs and I could see fear in their eyes. We agreed it was the altitude illness, but everyone wondered why this time the altitude had affected me so much when I had been there before without experiencing it. This altitude was not as high as that in Chile, where I had endured a worse reaction.

I knew that I was stressed and exhausted. I had worked for almost two years, working late and being the first and last in the office. I think I had burnout. Altitude sickness happens because there is less oxygen in the air that you breathe at high altitudes, and the wine could have made it worse. Then Mamo (Thembelihle's nickname, short name for Mamoyo), who was 14 years old, asked me for the first time about my job. 'Why are you working in the mining industry, Auntie? Isn't that a job for men? Sounds like a tough job. Why don't you work somewhere where it's easy and you don't have to stress?' I looked at her and smiled. But questions started pouring now from everyone, all curious as to why I had chosen mining in the first place, out of all the professions and industries. I was the odd one out in the family, having studied chemistry and worked in mining. The rest of my family either studied statistics, mathematics, finance or medicine. Even though I was skilled in mathematics, I still chose applied science at PhD level.

As I reflected on my career and leadership journey, I narrated my story to my family, who were all curious to know. I started from my childhood, with my sisters joining in the narration about how we grew up. My son, nephew and nieces were listening with curiosity as they had never met my father, who had died when he was only 52 years old.

Each day as we sat by the fireplace, I continued my story and shared my journey with my curious family, to the point where my son, nephew and nieces said I should write a book, as they found my story inspirational. They were amazed at the challenges I had faced as a woman in STEM, and inspired by the fact that I rose above those challenges and still loved the industry. They were shocked at how the mining industry contributes to the well-being of the world, making it a better place. They had no idea about the vast uses of most of the country's commodities and the extent of the contribution of the mining industry. Nor the fact that Africa has some of the most resources in the world. My sisters were also surprised about the uses of the platinum group metals (PGMs). By the end of the night, they had an appreciation of why I had stayed in the mining industry for 25 years, despite it being male dominated and with many invisible barriers for women. They previously had no idea about some of the challenges I faced and how I overcame them. We would talk sometimes but not in too much detail, as most of the times we met on holidays, we wanted to put work behind us. The next six days were filled with my stories of how I navigated the male-dominated workplace to succeed. I could see they were inspired, and I was motivated and encouraged by my family to write a book and share my success factors.

Patience with her family at Afriski in Lesotho in May 2018
(3rd from left)

At the end of the holiday, they all agreed that I had spoken with passion and they had learned a lot. We concluded that the world needs more women in STEM, and that leaders in male-dominated workplaces need to do more to remove the invisible barriers stopping women from succeeding. They jokingly suggested that maybe the sabbatical was a blessing in disguise, and I should share the knowledge with the world and inspire more women in STEM. At that moment, Thembelihle decided that she would now pursue her GCE Cambridge A levels in

STEM-related subjects and we encouraged her to follow her passion. When she later received her GCE O Level Cambridge results with five distinctions, she called me to say how my story had inspired her. She now understood how important STEM subjects are and the vast career opportunities they provide. She initially wanted to be a fashion designer and thought she could pursue both, but at university, she wanted to study chemical engineering.

After this discussion, I thought to myself that if I could inspire a young girl and open her eyes to the vast opportunities that STEM-related subjects can offer, imagine how many more girls or women I could inspire by publishing a book. In addition, I knew that the narrative of the mining industry needed to change, as people are not educated about what it is all about. But most importantly, if STEM professions will be needed even more, where are the women? I put the idea of writing a book aside at that time, but a year later, I was selected for the IWF Fellows Program in August 2019, and that idea came back—this time as part of my legacy project, and that dream became a reality!

A study by McKinsey Global Institute (Woetzel and Magdavhav 2015) found that women's economic equality is good for business. The study showed how advancing women's equality can add $12 trillion to global growth by 2025. Despite recent advances in trying to close the gender gap, especially in male-dominated workplaces and STEM professions, there are still few women interested in STEM subjects.

The United Nations has set ambitious goals for its 2030 agenda for sustainable development goals (SDGs), and specifically its goal 5 for gender equality. Empowering women in the economy and closing gender gaps in the world of work are mandatory to achieving this goal. In light of the impact of the COVID-19 pandemic and the rise of digital transformation and space exploration—or rather, space mining—there is a sense of urgency for a campaign to help women and in particular, those in STEM professions. However, there are still barriers that hold women back, including lack of female role models in the same field. The prominent barriers in male-dominated workplaces include gender biases and unequal growth opportunities (Beckton & Okzan 2012).

In 2018, there were 24 female CEOs on the Fortune 500 list, which is only 4.8% of all senior leadership positions. The most recent statistics from Catalyst Research (2021) show an increase from 1.2% to 6% of CEO positions held by women on the Fortune 500 list. Women are underrepresented in the C-Suite, receive lower salaries, and are less likely to receive a critical first promotion to manager than men. This is worse for women in STEM-related professions. COVID-19 exposed the vulnerability of women to the new future of digital transformation. A question often asked is whether women and men act all that differently. A book authored by Helgeson and Goldsmith (2018) on how women succeed concluded that there are certain habits that keep women from reaching their career goals. On the other hand, a study by Beckton and Okzan (2012) specifically on women in mining and, more recently, King (2020), have concluded that amongst other factors, the culture of an organisation is critical. Companies therefore can greatly benefit from increasing employment and leadership opportunities for women, which has been shown to increase organisational effectiveness and growth.

The question I reflected on most as I thought about writing my story was: What did it take me to succeed in a male-dominated workplace? What exactly moved the needle for me in my career, as I am often asked? Do I have a blueprint to navigate the common but sometimes subtle challenges of the mining industry? As I narrated my story to my family, I realised I can share some of these invisible barriers and create a blueprint for women to succeed. Most importantly, I can highlight where the male-dominated industry is failing women and what needs to be done.

An important factor in this is that women are being held back from achieving the highest leadership positions, which was the major barrier in my career. I have read many books, including *Lean In* (Sandberg 2013), *How Women Rise* (Helgesen and Goldsmith 2018), and *GRIT* (Duckworth 2017). I applied all the practical advice from these authors, and I attribute some of my success to insights I gleaned from their books. However, I believe it only works for people who look a certain way, are in a not so male-dominated work environment like mining, and at a certain level in a woman's career. To test this, I conducted a survey with over 100 women in STEM-related professions. I also interviewed 30 women across the globe to find out what it had taken for them to succeed. The most important insight in this book is my own experience, and I will share what worked and what didn't work throughout my leadership journey as a black woman in STEM, working in the mining industry.

There are also several female role models in STEM that have been celebrated for many years and continue to be, in certain media. However, I don't think we have done much to celebrate these women. For example, how many people know that Ada Lovelace, who was born in 1815, is the English mathematician who worked on the maths of the general-purpose computer? Consequently, she is the author of the first computer program. Another phenomenal woman in STEM, who inspired me after watching the movie *Hidden Figures*, is Katherine Johnson. Katherine Johnson was a US mathematician who retired from NASA in 1986 and did some calculations in orbital mechanics, leading to the success of the first US spaceflights. There are many others, but we don't hear much about their success stories—only about those of the males, hence my *why* in sharing my story: This story may not be about being a founder or inventor, but I hope it might inspire someone, somewhere, someday.

My mission with this book is therefore to help advance the United Nations' SDG5 in STEM-related professions by providing insights into the key success factors of navigating male-dominated STEM workplaces like mining. Secondly, to inspire and empower women to take on more STEM-related jobs and businesses. Lastly, to help policy makers/leaders make informed decisions about how to accelerate the pace of transformation for women and girls in STEM. As a woman in mining and STEM, I share my story of how I navigated the male-dominated work environment to become Africa's most influential woman in mining. I have also created strategies and tools that will help women who feel stuck in their careers. At the end of each chapter, you will find a summary link to free bonuses for women (and men) who aspire to be global leaders in STEM.

My story starts with how my upbringing shaped the trajectory of my life, and of how parents can influence their daughters. I talk about my journey in a male-dominated workplace, where I have met amazing people: mentors, coaches and sponsors. I speak about the role of the boys' club culture, especially in mining, highlighting it as one of the major barriers women face, and what leaders should be doing to help close the gender gap for women's advancement.

Firstly, the model is based on leading oneself. My experience attending many leadership and personal development programs across the globe shows that self-mastery is fundamental for anyone who wants to succeed in any career or business. Without mastering their emotions, understanding their values, and knowing who they really are, a leader can make poor judgments for the teams they lead. Knowing oneself helps a leader make wiser decisions. I have found that self-mastery starts with taking care of oneself. An example is having burnout and making not-so-sound decisions, which almost cost me my life.

Self-mastery is at the core of everything. The second part is having that spiritual *muscle*, which some would call mind power. Not having a source from which to draw when all physical sources are depleted can be detrimental. COVID-19 has made a lot of people start questioning the meaning of their lives. A leader's true colours are tested in a crisis. Who am I? What am I here for? Who am I serving? These were questions leaders were asking themselves. This book will show that my belief system, in conjunction with my values and drivers, played an influential role in my success.

Throughout my career, grit was one character trait that contributed to my success. How quickly do you bounce back after a setback? Besides the fact that the mining industry is male dominated, it is also a tough job. I found myself working late, travelling to remote places and not having enough time for my family. One needs grit to succeed, as evidenced by previous work by Duckworth (2017), which says passion and resilience are the key to success in anything. I tested this theory and indeed it is what made me successful in my early career.

A combination of courage, confidence, competency and having a strategy was the third essential factor. Leading oneself, knowing what you really want and having crystal clear goals are paramount. What are you known for? What are you the go-to person for? What would leaders discussing talent management say about you? Building a reputation as an expert in your early career is crucial. Working hard was second nature to me.

Relationships matter as you rise through the ranks to more senior roles. It is no longer just about what you do or about your competency and grit. All things being equal, women need to build relationships with whomever they work with. In a male-dominated work environment, it is often difficult as colleagues are mostly men, and women struggle with things like after-work drinks, as they have other commitments. I found it difficult to relate, and yet these social interactions are often where the most important conversations take place.

Advocating for what you want is still critical even when relationships are in place. This is where sponsorships come in, especially when one wants to be promoted. As much as companies have talent management strategies and talent mapping, the biggest challenge for organisations is talent attraction and retention. Influencing and advocating skills are important as this is how you build rapport with teams, stakeholders, and those you lead. How you show up and lead teams becomes critical. One of the vital skills I had to learn fast was the art of negotiation.

Having a learning mindset and constantly developing myself was an essential factor in my career progression. I went for a senior leadership program, and that was where I learned more about the art of negotiation. That was often what moved the needle. To succeed in any role, but especially in a male-dominated workplace, one has to be a great negotiator. It doesn't matter where you are in your career; if women are to break the glass ceiling, they need to learn how to negotiate.

I recall leading four major transactions where if I had failed to negotiate effectively, the company would have lost its license to operate. One occasion was just after a major incident in this company and the climate was not great. I had a supportive team that worked with me to get the deal done, but being clear on the mandate and what I could and could not concede was important. I was fortunate to have great female supporters in negotiating the deal. Needless to say, we succeeded and managed to get the deal signed with all approvals.

Leadership is at the core of talent attraction and retention for women in STEM. Without a vision or goal, it's difficult to navigate the complex work in a STEM-related profession like mining. Decisions for employees to stay and add value at whatever level are dependent on leadership. Leadership defines the culture of an organisation. As I moved up the ladder, I started having to influence the conversations both internally and externally on issues affecting women. New questions I pondered were: What are the leadership competencies required for the 21st century? What can we learn from some of the most successful female leaders who steered their countries through the COVID-19 pandemic?

Mining is the type of industry that employs mostly STEM-related professionals. You can have a love-hate relationship with it. You love it for the challenge, for the huge salaries and benefits, and there's never a dull moment. But you can easily hate it—for lack of a better word—for its male-dominated nature. You need to understand the history of mining, but most importantly, the uses of the products it produces. I sometimes think about how some people talk so badly about the industry without understanding that without the products it produces, the world could not function.

Finally, what is unleashing my superpowers? *Unleashing my superpowers* is a leadership concept with a call to action for every leader in male-dominated workplaces to empower more women to reach top leadership positions, thus helping close the gender gap. It takes having more women in leadership to close the gender gap, but most importantly, it takes male champions to move the needle. The concept is based on first leading self, then others, then business. I have summarised my leadership strategies on what it takes to succeed in a male dominated mining workplace with what I call the **Peak Performance Leadership Model**.

Knowing yourself is what gives you meaning. Ask yourself the difficult questions: What are my mission, purpose, and values? What am I here for? Once you know your gift to the world, use your voice as a force for good. What is your source of power? What is your anchor? When you have your power, how do you use it? Who do you impact? What do you want to be remembered for? What are you doing as a leader to honour someone's dreams, especially those of women? This is about overcoming adversity, understanding others and leading with authenticity, trust and compassion. When people you lead feel your energy, vibrating love, value for stakeholders naturally follows.

In a male-dominated workplace, you are guaranteed adversity, being spoken over, and being thrown under the bridge, but if you know your values, your mission, and what gives you meaning, you wouldn't put yourself in an organisation that doesn't value your contributions. You will have the foresight and intuition to join a community that has values aligned with yours, and your energy will attract that kind of organisation. Tap into your inner wisdom. You will know how to remove self-limiting beliefs, tune into who you truly are, be your authentic self and unleash your superpowers.

You know who you are, you are enough, and you have the courage to stand up for what you believe. You know how to take responsibility for yourself and not be a victim of circumstances. You know how to master the art of leading others compassionately while inspiring them. You know how to build peak performance teams and help them unleash their superpowers. Every person has this superpower within them.

Ultimately, unleashing your superpowers is using your voice. Use your voice for good, and raise it if you have to. If you're still not heard, go outside and use your voice with greater force. That is truly unleashing your superpowers. There is a time to lead and a time to follow, a time to succeed and a time to fail, a time to be confident and a time to be humble. Women have the superpowers they need to succeed and it's time to unleash them! *Wathinta umfazi, wathinta imbokodo* is a Zulu saying: You strike a woman, you strike a rock. This is particularly so as women reach C-Suite positions in male-dominated workplaces.

I hope that by the time you finish reading my story, you will have gained some insights into how it unfolded and taken away a valuable lesson from each turn. Let us all shine our lights and lead the way for others to shine theirs.

CHAPTER 1

OVERCOMING CULTURAL BARRIERS: THE LOST TRIBE OF THE LEMBA GIRL

*It isn't until you come to a spiritual understanding of who you are—
not necessarily a religious feeling, but deep down, the spirit
within—that you can begin to take control.*
— Oprah Winfrey

LOVE by Dr Patience Mpofu

What is your Why?
Why are you in existence?
The purpose of my life is to love and give love
The purpose of my life is impact
When you know your Why
Everything else flows
My Why is doing what I love, with love and passion
When you love what you do, rewards come flowing
My cup overflows with love

Love makes you forgive
Love is at the centre of everything
Love makes you get up without worrying about tomorrow
Love gives you purpose
My cup overflows with love

The secret to living a fulfilling life is to give love and expect nothing
What are you giving today?
What is your gift?
Do you love what you do with passion?
Does it give you meaning and purpose?
Love is indeed the highest energy frequency of all
Give love and light to all
My cup overflows with love

Introduction: The Birth of the Lemba girl

Our background—where we come from and how we were socialised from a young age—shapes our belief systems and plays an important role in who we become.

On a chilly Sunday morning on May 2, my parents, Stephen and Parto Nhongo, welcomed a daughter. They looked at each other and thought, *not another girl*. Despite their disappointment at having a third girl after praying to God for a baby boy, they quickly consoled each other. Hence, they named her Patience Nhongo Zhou. My name was meant to convince my father to be patient, as a boy would eventually come. My father was relentless about achievement and uplifting his family and community, but he had one desire that kept him awake: to have a baby boy. My mother already had my two sisters and me at the time. There was pressure from both sides of the family, but mostly from my father's side, for my parents to have a son.

When my parents gave me this name, I had no clue how much this name would test my ability to be patient throughout my life, especially working in a male-dominated work environment. Our given name is our very first social tagging and sometimes can be a self-fulfilling prophecy in our lives. As you read through all the chapters, you will see, in every stage of my life, I have been patient with people, situations or even myself.

Being patient requires persistence and mental and spiritual strength. Indeed, my parents were very patient, praying daily for God to give them a baby boy. Two years later, God granted their wish and my mother gave birth to a baby boy, Thembinkosi, a Zulu name meaning *Trust in the Lord*. Finally, my parents were happy, especially my father. This young child was adored more than all of us; it was as though a king had been born. Then one day, when I was about four years old, I heard screams followed by crying, and I could see many people coming to our house. All I heard was, 'Thembi is no more'. I didn't understand what was going on. No one spoke to us or told us what happened to Thembi. My cousin Prisca said he had left us and was now with God. I wanted to ask more, but as kids, death was a sacred thing that you didn't talk about. All we knew was that he was now with God in heaven. That was the beginning of a new chapter for my parents as they battled with the loss of their only son. Death comes as a thief in the night.

Later on, I understood why having a baby boy in my mother's generation was important. Culture made it so. A boy was more valuable than a girl. A son carried the family name, while a girl got married and left her family.

Thereafter, my parents struggled to have a second boy. In the quest to satisfy cultural norms, my father even married a second wife and, to his disappointment, was blessed with four more girls. My parents waited for over 17 years, with my mum having four pregnancies and painfully, three miscarriages, before she was blessed with another son. Talk about a strong woman! She balanced working in the city while taking care of all her children and extended family. In total, we are ten girls and two boys.

The death of my little brother was a defining moment, not just for my parents, but for my entire family. In the years to come, when my mother continued to have more children, it led to quarrels and fights with my father. Looking back, the dynamics of my parents' marriage may have impacted how I perceive marriage. Gender-based violence is real. I vowed to study and work hard so that I could be economically independent. My mother ended up staying, like many vulnerable married women, because she was not economically independent.

My parents had met at a nearby park and according to my mum, it was love at first sight. They were married two years later. Even though that spark of love had been instant, it took my mother six months to accept my father as a boyfriend. He tried several times to get her to accept his proposal as her boyfriend, but she wouldn't budge. We asked her what eventually made her accept him and she said my father was eloquent in English and he pursued her for more than six months without giving up. But what sealed the deal was the fact that he was from the Lemba tribe *(VaRemba in Shona)*. We asked why that was important as we didn't see the relevance of being a Lemba *(Muremba)*, or the meaning of it. She smiled and said, 'Don't you know the Lemba have an important and interesting history? They didn't originate from Africa but have roots from the Jews, and they built some of the greatest sights in Zimbabwe'.

Patience with her parents when she was less than a year old (front right)

The Lost Tribe: The Origins of the Lemba

We grew up in a Lemba tradition, which had a significant impact on our belief systems. Studies show that our belief systems drive our values and decision making. As I was growing up, I heard the word *Lemba* and learned what it meant and why it mattered. If you want to know someone deeply and understand what motivates them, get to know their story. It all starts with how we were socialised. How I was socialised may partly explain my motivation for choosing a STEM background and ultimately working in the mining industry. *How did you get into a male-dominated workplace like mining?* That is the question my family was asking me. 'Mining chose me!' is my answer.

My family and I would sit around the fire, chatting and laughing about our boarding school stories. My sister was a great storyteller; her stories were always full of humour. My grandmother would laugh, and we would ask her how she met our grandfather and what he was like. She would proudly say he was very tall, handsome and light skinned. She would emphasise the light skinned part several times as if that was so unique. You see, being light skinned was admired in some African cultures back then. Although I never knew him well as he had died at an early age, I often wondered about my grandfather. According to my grandmother, he was a respected teacher who came from a well-to-do family. He belonged to a tribe called the Lemba.

It was not until we were celebrating the 40th birthday of one of my sisters that we requested that our Uncle Simon Nhongo (my father's younger brother who worked for the UN for many years) tell us some history about our family, where we came from and the significance of the Lemba. This is when the journey of trying to understand my heritage began.

I acknowledge with gratitude the group of Lemba historians and my Uncle Simon Nhongo, who have put together this piece of work. Who are the Lemba? The Lemba are well documented in various books and published papers (Mullen 1969, Mourant and Sobczak 1978; Mandivenga 1983, Nyrop 1985, Mathiva 1992, Spurdle and Jenkins 1994, Thomas et al 1998, Parfitt 2000, Travis 2009).

To put historical matters into context, there are two competing versions of the historical and cultural origins of the Lemba. According to Professor Parfitt (2000), the Lemba originated in Jerusalem (Israel) and migrated to Sanaa (Yemen) following some upheavals in Old Palestine. Then, as succession conflict flared up after the death of Mohamed in 632 AD, they gradually migrated as traders (hence their praise name *Mushavi*) south-westwards to settle along the eastern coast and interior of South-Eastern Africa. It is believed that they initially established and settled in Mozambique (in 900 – 920 AD) at a place they called Sena (corresponding to Sanaa in Yemen where they had come from) among mostly indigenous Khoi-San and Bantu host communities. The latter had migrated earlier mostly from Central Africa to the pre-existing Monomotapa Empire, stretching from Western Mozambique and North-East Zimbabwe down to the communities along the north and south catchment areas of the Limpopo River (Parfitt 2000).

When the host Kingdom of Monomotapa initiated the construction of the great Zimbabwe monument, the Lemba (specifically the Tovakare Clan of which I am a member) were engaged as consultant architects and artisans to design and manage the construction works, using the architectural skills they brought with them from the Arabian Peninsula (Yemen). The Great Zimbabwe Monument was built between 1100 and 1450 AD. To back up this version of their history, the Lemba brought with them a replica of the Biblical Arch of the Covenant (Ngoma Lungundu), a remnant of which is on display at the National Museum in Harare. To further bolster this historical version of Lemba origins, genetic mapping was done to test the hypothesis that the Lemba are of Semitic origin. The results suggested that 50% of the Lemba Y-chromosomes are Semitic in origin, 40% are African, and the ancestry of the remainder is yet to be resolved.

The other version places the origins of the Lemba in Elmozaids of Oman, from where they migrated to Sanaa (Yemen) under the leadership of Suleiman and Zaid (Mullen 1969). Thereafter, they followed the same migration patterns as described above. While the first version claims that the Lemba have Semitic Jewish ancestry, the second version posits that the Lemba come from Semitic Islamic Arabs (Mullen 1969). The compromise between the two versions is that the roots of the Lemba are Semitic Jews and/or Arabs. Both groups of purported origin (Jews and Arabs) practise male circumcision, shun consumption of pork products and mice, and do not eat animals that have died on their own or are slaughtered without observing special cutting and bleeding procedures that adhere to halal or kosher principles.

To preserve genetic purity, the Lemba encouraged marriage within the broader Lemba groups across the 12 major clans, but generally discouraged Lemba women from marrying non-Lemba men. However, over the years, many Lemba women were married off to non-Lemba men (especially host communities' chiefs). In modern times, inter-marriage has become so widespread that it's no longer an issue.

There are four principal attributes of the Lemba culture that set them apart from the cultural practices of most indigenous communities that hosted them. As such, they were held in high esteem in the communities where they settled. The first was the initiation rite of male *circumcision*. This somewhat paramilitary practice was intended to instil discipline, courage and adherence to, or respect for, cultural mores. The second Lemba attribute was how relatively wealthy they were when they settled among host communities. One generic term for VaRemba and related clans, from when they settled in Zanzibar was VaMwenye (a Kiswahili term for *"owners of wealth"*. They were not only prosperous traders but also skilled artisans who worked in the mines that produced gold and other minerals (plus ivory) which they exchanged for beads, spices, cloth and jewellery from Arab and Portuguese merchants on the East African coast. Maybe this explains why I was drawn to the mining industry!

The third Lemba attribute was their strict adherence to shunning pork and associated kosher/halal protocols which impressed the host communities to the extent that some of them would invite Lemba "butchers" to slaughter their domestic beasts so that their Lemba neighbours could also participate in whatever communal festivities the animals were being sacrificed for. This kind of cultural discipline was held in such high regard by most of the host communities that they were co-opted into some of the Lemba cultural practices, including circumcision. When I was growing up, the ritual slaughter of animals and the taboo of eating pork were strong cultural tenets of my father. He and my grandfather never allowed pork meat in our house and my father always ate meat from a halal butcher.

The fourth attribute was *traditional medicine,* in which the Lemba were so highly skilled that the traditional leaders of host communities retained their services on a residential basis. Thus, Chief Mataruse of Mberengwa allocated my ancestor (Nhongo) a whole fertile valley to settle his relatives from Masase (where Nhongo migrated from). In return, some Nhongo maidens were married off to the chief and some of his relatives, thus breaking the Lemba practice of marrying only among themselves. There is also reference in literature to Lemba medicine men being retained in Lobengula's kraal from 1870 to 1894. Indeed, Lemba medicine men were so well known for their medicinal powers that their Shona neighbours eventually borrowed the name *Chiremba* to designate a modern-day doctor!

The majority of the Lemba are settled in South Africa, Zimbabwe and Nigeria where they are known as the Igbos. There are many prominent figures who have claimed to be Black Jews, including a well-known political leader in South Africa. Some recognition of the Lemba by the Jewish community is documented. The former President of South Africa invited several of the Lemba elders to Pretoria in 1999. After the visit, the Lemba became more recognised as an African Semitic tribe in southern Africa (Parfitt 2000). Many researchers believe the Lemba may eventually achieve their goal to be recognised as a lost tribe of Israel. Even though our original religion is assumed to be Judaism, most of the Lemba converted to Christianity, including my parents.

When people addressed my father or uncles, they were called *mushavi*. The above sets the context of my background as a *Mushavi or Musoni* (the girl believed to have some sort of Semitic background even though it's still to be validated). Whether it's proven or not, my family has always said that our generation of the Nhongo family is inclined towards STEM subjects.

How Family Values Shape Who We Become

How we are socialised shapes who we become. African norms start with the role of women and men in society. My parents' generation (and even my own generation in some African cultures) believe that men are superior to women in many ways. The husband pays *lobola* (dowry) and consequently, the woman belongs to the man's family. There are now debates about the role of lobola in the 21st century, which brings us to why it came about in the first place.

Women were encouraged to focus on marriage instead of pursuing careers. Marriage was a sacred thing, but in the 21st century, when women are fighting for equality in the workplace, why can't we redefine some of these cultural norms? My mother used to say that the man is the head of the house and the woman is the neck. She emphasised respect for both parties rather than just one.

I have always believed that marriage is sacred, and that two people define their own rules. They can decide how they want to raise their children; it shouldn't be prescriptive. But this was not so in the African context I grew up in. There was and still is no equality, and there were defined rules for women and men. Not so long ago, women were forbidden to work. Men were supposed to be the providers and women the nurturers. Women were not to work, especially in a male-dominated environment like mining. To have a seat at the table in a mining company as I did would have been taboo, to say the least. Marriage was and still is considered the most important achievement for women. When a woman gets to a certain age, aunties will ask the dreaded question: *When are you getting married?* I got that a lot until they got tired of asking. They eventually concluded that I was not the marrying type since I was doing a man's job.

Divorce in those days was unheard of. Painful as it might have been for both parties, it was deemed an embarrassment to the family because the man had paid lobola, so what would the family say? As a result, women stayed in abusive relationships for the sake of the family. This goes deep. Lobola was done with good intentions in that era. How should we update this cultural norm, and how relevant is it now, when we are talking about gender equality?

The role of unconscious bias therefore starts young. What is unconscious bias? It can be summarised as prejudice or unsupported judgments in favour of or against one thing, person, or group as compared to another, in a way that is usually considered unfair (Banaji and Greenwald 2013, Bohnet 2016). Some cultural backgrounds and religious belief systems accentuate discrimination against women. We see this in marriage and in the duties perceived to be for men and for women. Men no longer need to hunt, but women are still expected to cook, clean, wash the kids and do all the traditional domestic duties. Thank God for technology, but these old rules are still prevalent. This can carry on in the boardroom, where a woman—especially a black woman—is expected to serve tea for everyone.

My paternal grandfather was well respected as a teacher in the community. My grandmother, on the other hand, did not have the opportunity to be educated despite being smart. How she got married was not according to her will. As their families were herding cattle, my grandmother's family's cows ate the mealies (corn) in the field. As compensation, my grandmother was given to my grandfather in marriage at 12 years old. My grandfather did not want to marry her, so for over six years there was no sex between them. It was only after she turned 18 that she was allowed to be the lawful wife. She then gave birth to my father and aunt. While we are talking about life in Africa, this is still practised elsewhere in the world. UN Women reports that child marriages are still prevalent.

My maternal grandfather was well-known in his village in Nhema, Shurugwi. He had several wives and was known by the name Win. It's interesting how a name can be a self-fulfilling prophecy. My mum used to lament that my grandfather wouldn't pay for her to attend university in Zambia because he prioritised males over females when it came to education. She always said, 'I could have been a nurse or doctor had it not been for my father who didn't believe a woman can be educated.' My life is a testament to how far women in Africa have come.

There are many stereotypes that held women back in those days. My mother had fewer choices than I did. She was a devoted mother and worked tirelessly in a shop in the city, including on weekends. I watched my mother have all those children and go to work until almost full term during pregnancy. I kept thinking, *Why can't she stop? Why does she need a boy in the family?* The answer is: because girls were not valued as much as boys. A girl would get married and belong to the man's family and carry her husband's name, while a boy would marry and carry on the family legacy. That on its own is a cultural barrier. Maybe it worked in previous generations, but many things have changed, and women are now employed.

My mother eventually stopped working to take care of me and my siblings. She could have pursued a medical career and become one of the best doctors in the world for all we know. She encouraged us to work hard so that we could have financial freedom and not have to rely on a man. Forty years later, what my mum has contributed to society by raising great leaders is commendable.

There are many barriers for girls that start when they are young, particularly in developing countries like those in Africa, where most girls miss school due to having periods. In my view, this is a basic human rights issue, and no child should be left behind because of it. The right to dignity starts with the girl child. It's embarrassing for girls to go to school with inadequate sanitary protection. It should be made free to all girls around the world. For families who can't even afford food, sanitary pads are a luxury. The playing field should be level for girls; they should have access to such needs.

Women are often responsible for carrying out all the household duties, bearing children, and caring for the children and the extended family, and they are still expected to work. I saw this with my mum trying to juggle caring for all seven of us and, at the same time, working in a department store. I noticed my mother's swollen feet every day, but she was still expected to come home after work and cook for her family, clean, and get up the next morning for work.

My pursuit of a career that is very white and male-dominated was unheard of. When my mother learned that I was working in the mining industry, she flipped. First, I worked for a mining company, and then I got a PhD in mining, which was too much according to her and many other people. Even today, she laments that I should have been a nurse or doctor, not working in the mine. This is an example of the kind of unconscious bias our parents impose on us, that sits in our unconscious brain and makes us less confident. We need to start early if we are to remove these limiting belief systems.

Inclusion and diversity are essential to understanding these biases. People should be allowed to be who they want to be. Why should people be pigeonholed based on their sexual orientation or gender? We are spiritual beings and are all equal. I often prefer what are considered masculine interests, such as watching sports, reading about current affairs, and economics. But I also enjoy what are considered feminine interests, like cooking and chatting.

At some point I started becoming self-conscious, and I think the more people reinforce certain beliefs, the more the brain conforms to that belief system. Then there is the issue of colour. We were colonised in Zimbabwe by the British and somehow made to believe that black, or anything that was not white, was inferior. I remember growing up and idolising everything of European descent until I learned that we are all equal. The question is: does everyone believe we are equal in the workplace?

There is still more to be done, especially in developing countries. There are social norms that are regressing gender equality, such as mutilation and child marriages in African countries. These cultural barriers favour men. According to UN Women, female genital mutilation (FGM) comprises all procedures that involve altering or injuring the female genitalia for non-medical reasons, and is recognised internationally as a violation of human rights, and the health and integrity of girls and women. Although primarily concentrated in 30 countries in Africa and the Middle East, female genital mutilation is a universal problem and is also practiced in some countries in Asia and Latin America.

UNFPA estimates that there are an additional two million girls projected to be at risk of undergoing female genital mutilation by 2030. In response to this, the United Nations, through its UNFPA-UNICEF joint program, has been adapting interventions regarding female genital

CHAPTER 2

RISING ABOVE LIFE'S CHALLENGES WITH GRIT

You should never view your challenges as a disadvantage. Instead, it's important for you to understand that your experience facing and overcoming adversity is actually one of your biggest advantages.
– Michelle Obama

Now I Am the Voice, by Tony Robbins

Now I am the voice
I will lead, not follow
I will believe, not doubt
I will create, not destroy
I am a force for good
I am a leader
Defy the odds
Set a new standard
Step Up!

Why GRIT is Important

Duckworth (2017) has explored the secrets to success through her book *GRIT,* and concludes that when it comes to success, *grit is a combination of passion, resilience, determination and focus that allows a person to maintain the discipline and optimism to persevere in their goals even in the face of discomfort, rejection, and a lack of visible progress for years, or even decades.* This statement and these findings are very true as they speak to me. My early life and career is evidence of it.

In her extensive research, Duckworth (2017) firstly found that what mattered most was a never-give-up attitude. Improving the psychology of success, she found that being lucky and talented alone could not explain extraordinary success in any field. Instead, what differentiates success for the rising stars from those who drop out, is the ability and determination to keep going after failure. She says to be satisfied with being unsatisfied. This describes what has been my life path. There has never been any guarantee that life will be devoid of obstacles.

Success is a combination of passion and perseverance, and many would attest to that. This I found to be true as there are many people I know who are talented but have not been as successful as expected. By shining a spotlight on talent, we risk overlooking everything else. The most capable were not always the highest achieving. I remember a great friend of mine in primary school who was both smart and talented, but she never made it past high school, which was most unexpected of her. I have always been a hard worker and I believe this could have eventually become natural talent, while I believe my friend Felicity was naturally talented. She may have had the potential to be one of the greatest mathematicians for all we know. I have always wondered how this is possible. There are many factors that come into play. Given we had similar backgrounds, I used to wonder what else came into play for us to have contrasting differences in success.

We have an unconscious bias towards talent as observed by this study. Success is a series of unimpressive steps and that success and excellence are achievable through consistent effort. This has also been echoed in the book, *Think and Grow Rich*, by Hill (2014). Grit involves working on what you love. It involves not just falling in love but staying in love; there are no shortcuts to excellence. For some people, passion comes easily and they know exactly what they want to work on, from as young as five years old up until the day they die.

After reading *GRIT* and realizing that it played a huge role in success in my career, I decided to try learning how to swim. Since an incident when I almost drowned, I was afraid of water. This traumatic incident happened when I was in primary school, in third grade. I will never forget how I almost came to face death on that day.

It was one sunny day, and as usual just before we finished school, the weather suddenly changed with dark clouds gathering. Just when we were about to finish for the day, it started raining cats and dogs. My friends and I always loved naughty games such as playing in the rain water, pretending to swim when the water floods on the pavements and bridges. This particular day, despite all my friends refusing to go and play in the water, one bully girl who every girl feared as she was big and tall, insisted we all go and play in the water.

We had a communal swimming pool in our area and, occasionally, my sister and I would go and play there, but we were not good swimmers. This particular day, it rained very heavily and, little did we know, it was going to flood heavily on the bridges where we normally swim. As we were playing in the water, a huge gush of water came and, before we knew it, swept us and threw us uncontrollably. We all lost control and were swept separate ways. I remember being carried by this gush of water and screaming for help. I could smell death as a child. I was raised in a religious family, so I kept praying for God to save me: *Dear God, please save me. I do not want to die.* I tried to somehow swim, but my legs were not strong enough. Indeed, miraculously, God answered my prayer. My dress got caught on a big tree branch, and as I was being swept down the bridge, the tree became stuck by the bridge, and so did I. The water was gushing past me, but fortunately my head was afloat. This gushing lasted maybe a few minutes, but it felt like hours. I was in tears and was so scared, partly because I had almost died, but mostly because my left shoe and my bag were swept away. I was thinking about my mum and dad, and what I was going to tell them about what had happened to my new shoes and bag. I had swallowed all that dirty brown water and was throwing up.

I finally managed to dislodge myself and I climbed up the small bridge. I couldn't see my friends. I started walking towards home. As I arrived, I opened the door and my cousin Prisca was standing there watching in horror. 'What the hell happened to you? Where is your bag, and your shoe?' I just started crying. My mum was not yet back from work. She quickly took me in and helped me shower and change. I was waiting for a good beating from my mother and father. When my mother arrived, Prisca related what I had told her. Surprisingly, my mum was compassionate and was even worried if I was okay. I had a few bruises here and there, but I was fine. From that day, I never wanted to be near water. We would travel to nice places where there were lovely pools or beaches in South Africa, but I wouldn't swim or get near the sea. I always missed out on the fun. I didn't participate in any swimming lest that same incident happened—until 2018, when I decided it was time to face my fears.

After taking a sabbatical leave when my role became redundant in 2018, I was ready to learn and try new skills and hobbies. Learning how to swim was on my to-do list. My other sister, Diana, who lives in Johannesburg had had a couple of lessons and could swim but not confidently. She had started lessons when I decided to try swimming, so she encouraged me to join her. I kept postponing it until, one day, I just decided I wanted to do this. I was going to travel to many places, spending six months in Bali writing this book at some resort area with nice beaches. I was planning to sell my investments and pack and go. I soon realised though, that I was not going to enjoy it as I should, and I reminded myself that Bali is known for many tsunamis. After watching the move, *The Impossible*, where many people died in a tsunami in Thailand, learning how to swim became a must and not simply a nice *to-do*.

The lessons started in Australia when I visited my other sister, Zodwa. Learning to swim was one of the scariest and most difficult things I had to learn as an adult, apart from learning a new language and driving a car. Thank God, there were many adults in that swim school. Day one was excruciating. Day two was no different from the first day. The swimming instructor was very patient and really nice. We had our kickboards. What I hated was the water getting into my nose. I just couldn't get the hang of it. Then having to kick and trying to float was just so difficult. It was such a weird feeling. I felt like a dumb person. To make matters worse, we were training next to the kids, including my niece Malaika, whose ages ranged between three and seven years old. Some were in advanced classes. I felt so stupid, but I wasn't about to give up. This was in September 2018. I set a target that in six months' time, I should at least be able to swim five laps with ease, both freestyle and backstroke.

I continued the swimming lessons in 2019, until I could at least swim without a kickboard. By the time I went to South Africa in February, I could swim a full lap, but the breathing was still difficult. I continued the lessons with a lovely lady, Kaira, at Virgin Active Alice Lane in Sandton, until I could do four laps. I could now swim well, especially when doing the back stroke, but freestyle was still not perfect. If you want to succeed, you need to create new habits and break old ones. Being consistent with my training was critical. I was determined, and by the time I got to six months, I was able to swim at least four laps freestyle and six laps doing the backstroke. That was an achievement. I decided to set new targets. This time, it was ten laps. Slowly but surely, I was confident and could complete ten laps with ease. This went on with me setting new targets every time, until I could easily swim 30 laps. As I write this book, I can now do 30 laps freestyle in a 25 metre-long pool in 30 minutes. Each time I reached my target, I would reward myself with a two-hour massage.

This is what grit is all about—being passionate about something and setting goals to achieve—but most importantly, persistence and determination are essential. I almost gave up in the early stages of the training. It was hard, and sometimes I felt like I was not progressing, but I kept pushing and being consistent. The other thing I did was have a buddy and a role model. Diana was my buddy and role model. We trained together twice a week, at the same time and same place, in Bryanston, Virgin Active. So in this instance, grit was central to success and is similar to my early career days.

We undertook a survey of 100 women to see if grit is indeed the key to success for getting to C-Suite in male-dominated workplaces (STEM). The results were very interesting. We wanted to find out what it takes to get to C-Suite, if it is having a higher level of grit. The results showed that having grit is not the only factor as there was no difference in the grit score for specialists, managers, and C-Suite women leaders. The only interesting finding was that entrepreneurs scored higher on the grit score versus those in academia and those in corporate. The conclusion was that there is no linear relationship that, from specialist to C-Suite, the grit scores increase. However, C-Suite had a higher score than those in lower positions, although it was not very conclusive. A short executive report on this work can be downloaded from my website at www.unleashingmysuperpowers.com/bonuses.

The power of determination and grit was something I had within me as I was growing up. Education and working hard was very important, and this discipline was instilled in us from a young age. I made friends easily and immediately became drawn to the smartest girls in class. My father always said, 'Why hang around shuro?' *Shuro* is an animal that is not so clever. One thing I knew for sure was that I was brilliant in Maths. Being Lemba came with expectations that you excel in class, especially in Maths and Science. In primary school, when it was just the three of us, my sisters didn't disappoint, as they always got 100% from Grade 1 to 7 for all their subjects, while I, on the other hand, would pass with sometimes 99%.

That was not good enough. I remember, from grade 1 to 5, somehow I was always sixth or seventh in the class. This was because the top five or six kids would get 100% and I, for some reason, would get 99%. Both my sisters won prizes for being excellent in class many times, and I was the only one who never received a prize during prize giving. Our school used the system of giving overall numbers based on pass rates. In my mind, I knew my class had the brightest kids, but who do you tell that cares to listen? I was so determined to get a prize and I worked so hard.

This was the beginning of being labelled *average* by relatives who, when visiting us, would first ask, 'Did you pass?' The next question would be, 'What number?' Then I would stammer and try to explain before being cut off by my sisters or cousin who would tell them that I was perhaps eighth in the class. The relative would say, 'Are you playing at school? Your sisters are all number 1, and you on the other hand are number 8? This is not a Lemba!' I would shy away and feel frustrated, and would end up not explaining as the relative would have no interest in seeing my report, to see that I actually only missed out on being first in the class by 1%.

Now as an adult, I realise how an education system can create or make school children worse than they actually are by labelling kids and assigning them placement numbers. I really wasn't average, but it became a known thing that I *was* average in school. Somehow, in my mind, I knew how wrong this was but decided from that day that I did not want to be average. You will see as you read further that whatever I did, I wanted to do better than before. That started the journey of personal growth and self-improvement in my adult life. I was striving to be in first place, and this finally happened when I was in grade 6. That was a breakthrough. It was a tie with my best friend, Felicity, who was always first in class, and with a bright boy, Elias. Now came prizegiving day, which was always a secret beforehand.

Teachers never told anyone until the day before, and then the teacher would inform the prizewinners to prepare and to attend a rehearsal at the assembly. Parents were invited to witness the best of the best being awarded prizes, which of course, was purely academic. No prize was given for sports excellence or anything else, which I found so ridiculous. Anyway, there were two prizes to be given in our class. I assumed the three of us would be given the prize, so both my friend and I were so excited. The day before prizegiving, to my surprise, Elias and I were the only ones chosen for rehearsals. I was shocked and surprised as my friend was not included. She asked me if I had been called, and I had to be honest with her and told her I had been called. That didn't please her and I tried to encourage her to speak to the teacher. I can't remember what excuse the teacher gave her—something to do with character. I felt like a fraud, as deep down I always thought Felicity was the smartest, because she had been in first place from grade 1 to 7 and I had to work harder to get to that coveted first position. These are some of the belief systems that haunted me later in my career, where I felt as though I was not good enough, or like a fraud.

High school was another place where discipline and hard work were the order of the day. Felicity and I did not go to the same high school. I went to a boarding school, Ingwenya Mission (John Tallach) in Ntabazinduna, where grit was the culture and you had no choice but to fit in and focus on working hard and passing with high grades. John Tallach was (still is) known as one of the best secondary schools in Zimbabwe. There was no time to play, and sports was not big. You either had to go to church or study. It was a strict school and we were not allowed parties or discos. It was purely study and the competitive environment. We were told at school: 'Study hard so that you can go to university, then work even harder and your career and success is guaranteed.' I did as I was told, worked hard and passed with six distinctions and two Bs. I was one of the highest amongst the girls, and fifth in the entire school. My future looked bright. I began visualising my future.

I had gone to visit my grandmother after the results were announced. I was so happy. Finally, the hard work had paid off. I was feeling like a genius in maths and I enjoyed solving problems. My mother wanted me to be a nurse. My father said I could be anything I wanted to be. All I knew was that my life would never be the same again.

I met my friend, Felicity after receiving our results, who hadn't achieved so well. I always wonder, if she had been persistent and attended my school, would her outcome have been the same, or could she have performed better? For me, an environment that is nurturing, supportive, and has role models played a key role, but most importantly, it was grit. Felicity indicated that she didn't study as hard as I had, and she had attended parties with few hours for study. She had passed five subjects with mostly Cs. This was shocking to me as she was one person I always looked up to and thought was super smart. I had sisters who had done very well and they set the standard for me. Had I gone to other schools, what could I have become?

Patience after obtaining her GCE O-levels results

Felicity had natural talent, but I think she lost the passion and was not sufficiently persistent. Working hard and having smarter sisters and a supportive family helped me to get to first position in the class and ultimately to winning a prize. It just shows how having a strong self-belief and the pain of being labelled average motivated me to work harder with grit to finally succeeding. Therefore, in my view, grit is indeed the key to success—but to what extent in particular when it comes to career advancement to C-Suite in male-dominated workplaces?

Our beliefs also shape our resistance. Self-belief is important in succeeding in a career, and can actually be empowering. My personal experience in having a strong self-belief system helped me to take big risks that led to my career success. It helped me to have a sense of optimism, and to create resilience. As seen in the next chapter, this ability to weather setbacks and failures, without giving way to paralysing doubt, is critical for success. No-one can take away that belief system about self. The image you hold about self is critical. People will try to put you down and make you feel as though you are hopeless and useless, but if you believe in your abilities—and most importantly, have faith in the face of adversity—you will succeed. It's about mastering your core beliefs and never questioning yourself when you walk into a room and own it.

There was a time when I underplayed my intelligence, and of being smart and knowledgeable. I wanted to accommodate male egos, literally making myself appear ignorant and not smart. You would be in the wrong organisation, or have the wrong friends or associates, if you have to downplay your talents. If you have to be apologetic for your successes, then you are also in the wrong place. Stop being apologetic for your talent. You owe it to yourself to unleash your superpowers. Stop putting your head down for fear of being victimised, and so that you make the ego-driven leader feel good about themselves. It is time to unleash your superpowers. Smart people are sometimes called misfits. They don't fit in, because they are gifted with infinite intelligence. Steve Jobs didn't fit in, and there are many so-called misfits.

I was glad when I finally passed my GCE A-levels and was going to university. Finally, I would be out of my parents' home and starting a new, independent life. I wanted to be a medical doctor, but career choices were limited. I thought maybe a lawyer. I eventually settled for applied chemistry as I was a very curious person. I also thought there would be many more career choices with a STEM degree than being a lawyer. I saw how both my sisters' lives changed when they finished high school. They both studied maths for their postgraduate studies. They had freedom and even holidays and they were working part time, so they finally didn't have to run my dad's errands. You can understand how much I couldn't wait to also go to university.

University life was exciting. I attended the National University for Science and Technology (NUST) in Bulawayo. It was the second largest that time and we were pioneers of that university when it opened. I was so happy as there was no need to wear uniforms, and we could go to parties. I was staying at the university residence. All was good. I communicated again with my friend, Felicity who was studying to be a secretary. We immediately reconnected and would go out together. One day, she invited me to go with her to Zambia. Her cousin, who had spent many years in the United Kingdom, was getting married back in her home country in Zambia. I was excited about the idea of travelling regionally. We used to travel with my dad to Botswana, but this time it would be different. It would be me and my best friend. Felicity and I decided that we were going to use the train from Bulawayo, cross the border and go all the way to Victoria Falls. From Victoria Falls, we were going to Livingstone. From Livingstone, we would then catch another train to Lusaka.

I was so excited, and I went to speak to my mum and my dad. My mum was not happy but I insisted, until both of them conceded. Our trip was amazing, including a stop at Victoria Falls where we toured. It is about 380 km from Bulawayo to the north and is one of the world's most spectacular and largest waterfalls, located about midway along the course of the Zambezi River, at the border between Zambia to the north and Zimbabwe to the south. Its roughly twice the height of North America's Niagara Falls and well over twice its width. The Mosi-oa-Tunya (means the smoke that thunders) as it is commonly called is the world's greatest sheet of falling water world heritage for any avid tourists as described by UNESCO (UNESCO website). I have been to the Victoria Falls more than five times to a point of even doing a bungy jumping. Each time I visit, it feels fresh and I am in awe of its beauty.

We arrived in Zambia the following day and we cooked a lot of food for the family. There was so much that was happening, including a kitchen tea party that we attended. We enjoyed it to the point where we missed our transport to take us back to where we were staying so we decided to hitchhike. Shortly, a middle-aged man stopped for us. My friend was sitting in the front seat and the man started asking her name and if she would like to go clubbing. We told him that we have arrived where we need to be and he should stop the car, but he drove on past, without stopping. We were scared. We'd had a way of communicating since primary school whenever we were in danger. I tapped her on the shoulder and she knew that meant: *Danger, run!*

The moment the man stopped the car at a traffic light, we just opened the doors and ran. We ran as fast as lightning till we arrived home. Whether the guy was just playing games or what, the point is that he didn't stop and we didn't feel safe. Could we have been abducted? We will never know, but it shows how easy it is for that to happen to young girls when hitchhiking. It could have happened anywhere in the world. Girls, especially in Africa, disappear daily, and no one knows where they are taken, but research suggests they are taken across borders. How does the trafficking take place, most people wonder? Child and girl sex trafficking is one of the biggest challenges in the world. More than a million girls are trafficked daily according to the UN. Human trafficking is the process of trapping people through the use of violence, deception or coercion, and exploiting them for financial or personal gain.

* * *

Life doesn't prepare you for the unexpected; it's how you choose to deal with it that matters. I was back at university on a particular day and I woke up feeling very emotional but didn't know why. The previous night, I had spent time with my family at a restaurant enjoying ourselves. I slept very late. It was raining and you could smell the freshness of the rain in the air. I started crying for no reason. Something was amiss. I couldn't eat and I didn't want anything. I just knew something was not right. When I arrived at the university (the campus was far from where we lived, so we had a bus transport us), and I started doing my chemistry distillation experiments, I was shaking and I broke the distillation apparatus. The research lady was very kind and she asked me to take a seat and rest. I was sobbing uncontrollably when I heard my name being called by one of the lecturers.

My family had come to ask for me. I didn't ask what the problem was, but my eyes were filled with tears. I just knew it was death. I could see death in their eyes. Indeed, as we were approaching home, I said, 'Its Dad, isn't it?' They said yes. I lost my voice, my eyesight… everything. He had never been sick in his entire life. He was full of life and was just starting out as an entrepreneur. I cried so hard, my voice was gone. My younger brother was four years of age. My mother was then unemployed. I had all these siblings and extended family that looked up to my father. Who was going to take care of everyone now that he was gone? I was heavy with child. When I saw all my sisters, we just cried. I can never forget this day. Death was never something we experienced apart from my brother who was very young when he died. This time it hit hard. My father had a car accident. He fell asleep at the steering wheel. His car then swerved to the far left when he suddenly woke up and realised he was off the road. He must have turned the steering wheel too far to rectify, and the car went over the bridge. He died of internal injuries. As I write this, it still feels very fresh, as his death was so sudden. He was only 52 years old. Such is life. Death comes like a thief in the night.

My two older sisters and I had to grow up quickly and help my mother financially to take care of my nine siblings. Balancing life as a young mother, wife, and sister, and completing university, was one of the most challenging times of my life. The birth of my son was transformational. I was very young, only 21 years old, but there is that instant motherhood instinct that kicks in when you suddenly have a child while you are young. I had all the support from both my ex and my family. He was the first grandchild. I had to deal with having lost a father and with motherhood. I had no time to feel sorry for myself. All I knew was I needed to pass my university exams.

It is important to have a vision and never lose focus. The death of my father left a huge emptiness, fear and pain in me. However, despite this setback, I never lost sight of my goal, which was to obtain my honours degree. It was not easy, but I invested every ounce of strength that I possessed—physical, mental, and spiritual—towards my studies. In difficult situations such as these, you need strength not only from family support but from the power of the source of everything: in my case, the spiritual world. I am a Christian and was raised as such, so my belief in the Holy Spirit has always helped me cope with adversity.

I was doing well… I had picked up the pieces and I was managing to juggle being a university student, a mother and a wife. I had set goals for myself to succeed. Through determination and hard work, I achieved a distinction for work experience exams during my internship and, subsequently, achieved another distinction for my final year honours project, resulting in an overall upper second (2.1) grade for my degree, despite my father having just passed on. I learned that every fall does not mean failure.

Most people struggle to deal with unexpected events, especially with COVID-19, which was one of the most distressing periods of our lives. Rebounding after a setback requires resilience. We all have to face difficult moments in our lives. Proper training for our minds, bodies, and emotional resilience is important in confronting life's challenges. What is resilience? It is the ability to deal with setbacks. The more resilient we are, the easier it will be to pick ourselves up and get back to what gives meaning to our lives. The death of my father left us with an instant family of more than 30 people he was supporting, and we had to find ways to help each and every person who was dependent on him, including our own siblings. My mother always taught us to put others first. I was only 21, with a young baby and with an unemployed mother who was at the time still coming to grips with the death of my father. She was suffering from depression. The three of us, myself and my two older sisters, had to strategise together. We agreed to prioritise the education of our siblings. Unfortunately, the pension that my father left was not sufficient to even pay for any of their fees. I was getting a pocket money allowance from university, and that went towards helping.

* * *

1994 was a defining moment for everyone: the Mandela moment. Nelson Mandela was a hero globally but more so for every African person. I was fascinated by his eloquence, his courage and conviction. In my opinion, he is indeed the greatest leader of all time. I have read all his books and still refer to some of his teachings. He preached love and reconciliation. It is said that Mandela is one of few people with a high consciousness. All was well, and life was good again. I had moved to South Africa, was married and happy again. I now had a good job working as a research chemist at one of the second biggest platinum mine producers, Impala Platinum in South Africa.

Then, in 1998, another setback hit me… I became divorced. This was another traumatic experience in my life. Not only did I have to fend for myself and my son as a single parent, but I had to continue assisting my family in their upkeep. I had two choices: stick my head in the sand and feel sorry for myself, or dust myself off and get on with life so that I could achieve the goals I had set for myself. I had a son and a family to think about. There was no time to feel sorry for myself. I chose to remain focussed on my goals. I had to quickly shift the paradigm of being a victim to being victorious (being responsible). In life, as Mandela said, it's not how many times you fall that matters, it's how quickly you get up and dust yourself off and move on. Life is filled with unexpected events that you cannot control, but you can control how you respond.

No problem is ever permanent. The divorce made me realise that setbacks are only temporary and can drive you or destroy you. What drove me was knowing what I wanted in life. I knew I had a purpose and I had clarity for what I wanted to achieve this time. I had a son and family to look after, including the whole village that I had to help uplift from poverty. I couldn't let them down. During that time (2000), my career in the mining industry had already started. I was working as a senior chemist. I was struggling to make ends meet as the rent was expensive, and I had huge expenses every month; I was just getting by. Luckily, my aunt from the UN always used to visit her children who were attending boarding school in the Eastern Cape. She would always ensure she bought enough groceries that would last me for a long time. That was indeed a blessing as I knew my expenses were covered. I was working hard and would drive to Springs, as I was working in the labs. I had to drop off my son in the mornings in Benoni, then pick him up afterwards.

Towards year end, my friend Cindy and I (with whom I worked in the same lab) decided to do an MBA at WBS. We both applied and she got placed first. That time, I was acting in a more senior position and had spoken with my boss about a promotion. I had done very well and had presented great results for the research work I was doing. I presented every quarter on the research project on a new instrument that we had just commissioned, the research was in collaboration with a German consulting firm. I was developing new standards so that we could switch to the new technology that was faster and more accurate than the traditional method.

While I was waiting for both my MBA and promotion, I attended an interview with one big chemical company for a global leadership acceleration program. I was one of the four leaders accepted into the program. We were to be trained over two years, including getting a master's degree. I was ecstatic. My prayers had been answered. The power of faith and belief in breakthroughs was something I was used to. I always resort to the spiritual realm when things don't make sense.

Power of the mind is unbelievable. After the divorce, I kept saying, 'I wish I could go overseas for a while,' and I kept asking myself, 'How do I go overseas? How can I get a job overseas for a change?' As they say: ask and it shall be given. Indeed, God answered my prayers.

As if that blessing wasn't enough, one day, I had just finished lunch when I received a call at my office from an unfamiliar voice. The person on the line said, 'Hi Patience, this is Professor Ralston. I would like to congratulate you for winning the scholarship award to study for a PhD in Australia…' The rest I didn't hear, except when he mentioned Anglo Platinum.

I said, 'Sorry, I didn't get that.'

He repeated, 'I would like to congratulate you again that Anglo Platinum has decided to co-sponsor you.' My heart was expanding with excitement. I was ecstatic, to say the least. I couldn't believe that I had been praying for a job at Anglo Platinum, and had been rejected three times for positions I had applied for, and here they were offering to sponsor me to study in Australia.

My clients that I coach always ask, 'How do you deal with rejection?' I have reflected on how many times I have actually been rejected, and on the emotions associated with it at the time. Some of the worst rejections I have previously experienced made me question my abilities, and sometimes I would wallow in a self-pity party. But then fast forward to now, as I look back at my life, and I realise that some of the rejections were actually redirecting me to something bigger and more powerful. We face different types of rejection. It's about how you deal with the rejection that matters, and the meaning you give it. You can wallow in self-pity for a long time, and focus on why it happened, or you can choose to reflect on the learnings, and reframe the rejection as an opportunity for better things to come. Reframing helps me to keep focused on my mission. This was a typical case where the same company that had rejected me three times was coming back with triple the great dosage. A lesson here is that your current situation is not your final destination.

I thought I was dreaming when the professor said this. I asked for his number in case it was a hoax. He gave me his number and mentioned that I would be receiving a call from Anglo Platinum shortly, to arrange for a meeting so that they would know what my needs were and what the conditions were for the sponsorships. The moment he said goodbye, and I put the phone down, I screamed! I couldn't believe what had just happened! *Is this true? What if this is too good to be true?* I asked myself. Then as I was still making sense of what had just happened; indeed, a call came through. 'Hi, this is Sarah. I am phoning from… I would like to congratulate you first and foremost. We need to schedule a meeting between you and Sandy Lambert and Peter Charlesworth this week. When are you available?' The date was locked in and at 8 am on the appointed day, I was in the offices of Anglo Platinum, at the Anglo Platinum Research Centre in Germiston.

I was introduced to the HR person dealing with my case, Peter Barnes. I entered the boardroom where there were three directors and the HR Manager. It felt like a job interview. I was sweating as I could still not believe what was happening. They congratulated me and welcomed me to the family. *Is this a movie or something?* I was in a trance, and just listening. They took me through the sponsorship and details. We signed the agreement, but before that, they said there was one condition: I needed to resign from my current employer as there was a conflict of interest, and I should do this immediately. I told them there was no problem and that I would do so, but I needed to complete the project I was working on. They then put in the agreement date for when the sponsorship was effective.

Opportunities, when they come, come in droves. There was something about the brand in Africa that drew many people to Anglo Platinum. I had visualised myself working for this global company and now that dream had come true. I had the task of preparing for my trip to Australia, but before that, I had another task before me, which was to decline the offer from the other company. Despite my desire to be with Anglo Platinum it was still a difficult decision for me to make because the job that was offered seemed amazing. I consulted as usual with my two sisters Peddie, Pepsi and my mum, and we debated about it. My mum thought it was too soon as I had just divorced and it was too many changes all at once.

Eventually, what both my sisters said was that I have to think about what it is that I want—what's best for me at this point in time—but also I should think about the long term. What does the future look like for myself and my son? I had a lot to think about, but it was ultimately a no-brainer because I knew I wanted to go to Australia and I wanted to join Anglo Platinum. Eventually, I made the decision that I was going to Australia. It was a big decision. I would be joining the number-one platinum mining company in the whole world. I was ready for a new life, new beginnings and new friends. I knew it was what I had always wanted. But I wasn't sure about doing a PhD at that point in time.

Finally, I received the dual scholarship from the University of South Australia and this global mining company to study for a PhD. I started packing some of my things and giving away what I didn't need. When I went to see my boss, Dawn Stephens, she said she also actually wanted to speak to me about something. She told me the company had decided to pay for my MBA studies and promote me at the same time.

I was shocked and didn't know what to say to her. *Should I tell her that I'm actually resigning?* I decided not to, and waited until I had a student visa. Eventually, I had to tell her that I was resigning. I felt bad, but she was very supportive and said, 'Look, if I was in your position, I would've done the same thing. It's a great experience and you are going to learn new things; you're going to a new country.' That made it easier for me.

The student visa took much longer than expected. Eventually, I received it and my ticket was ready. I was leaving South Africa for Australia. As I arrived at the airport and boarded, I had mixed feelings as I didn't know what to expect. I was wondering what Australia would look like. I was excited but missed my family already, especially my son. I was going to start a new chapter in my life, in a new country with new people and a new career—potentially, my new life was about to begin. My hard work and persistence had finally paid off amidst all the turmoil. This dual scholarship to study a PhD overseas, was an opportunity of a lifetime.

Exercise

I believe being grittier definitely has played a huge role in my success this far. Grit has two components: passion and resilience. That's why, as a leader, when your teams lose passion, you need to worry. Passion is the burning desire to succeed. Have you seen how certain people have great talent, but when you speak to them about what they can do, they just don't have any enthusiasm or passion? Passion for me is like fuel. I will talk in detail in the next chapter about finding your passion, because if you are not in a career that lights you up, then your grit will be low and you will struggle to achieve your goals. Passion makes it easier to be resilient. When you are met with setbacks, you must not let them derail you.

You can find the grit scale that Duckworth (2017) developed, which measures your grit score, in her book, *GRIT*. Measure how GRITTY you are.

CHAPTER 3

HOW TO OVERCOME
IMPOSTER SYNDROME

*'My mother had a saying: Kamala, you may be the first to do many
things, but make sure you're not the last.'*
– Kamala Harris

Gratitude, by Dr Patience Mpofu

*No one is born with everything
Even the richest still wants more
Even the healthiest wants more
Even the prettiest or most handsome want more
Even the most powerful wants more
But in the wanting more, know that there is someone
Someone yearning for the basic needs of humanity
Gratitude is the way to infinite intelligence*

*Wait, have I lost what I had?
I can't believe I had the best health
I didn't realise I had an income
I didn't realise I had so much love
I had it but didn't appreciate it, until it was gone
That's the power of gratitude
Today give gratitude to what you take for granted
Think abundance and not lack*

Think giving and not wanting
Gratitude is the way to infinite intelligence

I am thankful for everything, everyone
I am thankful even to those who have given me pain
Without pain, there is no growth, there is no gain
Thank you for putting me in this situation
Thank you for giving me enlightenment
Gratitude is the way to infinite intelligence
Gratitude is indeed the key to happiness

Australia is a sovereign country comprising the mainland of the Australian continent, the island of Tasmania, and numerous smaller islands. It is the world's sixth largest country by total area and has a population of about 26 million. The capital is Canberra, and its largest city is Sydney. The country's other major metropolitan areas are Melbourne, Brisbane, Perth, and Adelaide. Australia is ranked one of the best places to live in the world according to *Business Insider*. This was based on an assessment of the best democratic countries to move to after the pandemic. Three Australian cities also made the top 10 most liveable cities. It has great access to education, with high life expectation and socioeconomic well-being. There are many great tourist attractions, such as the majestic Uluru, the Sydney Opera House, and some of the greatest beaches in the world, including Bondi. It has some of the best wines in the world, the world's largest living structure with its huge area of diverse organisms: the Great Barrier Reef is a must see. I would definitely recommend Australia as one of the best countries to visit.

According to the Minerals Council Australia, mining in Australia has been a significant primary sector industry and contributor to the Australian economy through its provision of export income, royalty payments and employment. Australia produces 19 useful minerals in significant amounts, from over 350 operating mines. Australia is one of the world's leading producers of bauxite (aluminium ore), iron ore, lithium, gold, lead, diamond, rare earth elements, uranium, and zinc. Australia also has large mineral sand deposits of ilmenite, zircon and rutile. In addition, Australia produces large quantities of black coal, manganese, antimony, nickel, silver, cobalt, copper and tin. The mining industry GDP increased 4.9 per cent in 2019–2020, and totalled $202 billion. This also made mining Australia's largest industry, with a 10.4 per cent share of the economy (Minerals Council Australia website).

My flight landed in Perth, Australia early in the morning the next day. I slept throughout the night. On arrival, I had to catch a connecting flight that was leaving in two hours. I quickly picked up my luggage and was so impressed by the efficiency and thoroughness of the staff. We had to go through the usual customs and immigration. 'Next please,' the immigration officer summoned me. I went straight away and gave him my passport. He looked at me smiling. 'G'day, how a ya?'

I said, 'Sorry, I didn't get that?' He ignored me and went on to stamp my passport.

'Is it y firs tym he?' I guessed he had asked *Is this your first time here?* I couldn't get the hang of the Aussie accent.

I said loudly, 'Yes, and I am so excited.'

'Y studen?' I thought about that… Okay, he is asking, *Are you a student?*

I said, 'Yes.'

I was thinking, *God, I thought English was the same. This surely is not the English I know. This is Australian English.* I quickly made my way to the bus, which took us to the domestic terminal. I was feeling sick and hot. It was in April 2000, but the heat was unbearable. I made my way to the check-in desk and checked in my luggage and then there I was at the domestic terminal waiting to board. In less than 30 minutes, we were boarding. As I sat on my seat, I realised I really missed home. I woke up with a start when I heard someone say, 'Ma'am, please may you make your way out. We have landed.' I realised I had slept throughout the flight. I was finally in Adelaide, a relatively small capital city in the state of South Australia, a gateway to some of Australia's best wine country.

I landed in the late evening and noted that the airport was much smaller than even some of the airports in South Africa. As I lay in bed in my room in North Adelaide, I reflected on what lay ahead. I was here to do a PhD, and had left my job, my family, and friends. I slept like a log until the next afternoon. I had serious jetlag. I went back to sleep and slept until midnight. I had the whole weekend to recuperate.

I arrived at UniSA and the former Ian Wark Research Institute (known as The Wark, which is now incorporated within the University's Future Industries Institute). The Wark was founded in 1994 and was one of the major research institutions in UniSA. This university is ranked 25th among the world's top young universities and is a top-ranking university in Australia for quality education.

The Wark established a reputation for solving complex industry problems through the application of excellent science and technology. A major function of the institute was the education of graduate students, and it had a highly prized international reputation in postgraduate education, with an outstanding graduate employment record. When I started my PhD, there were approximately seventy research students in The Wark who worked with research staff, ranging from junior to senior personnel. The Wark offered PhD and master's degrees by research programs in applied science and engineering. The Wark combined academic rigour and inquiry and was driven by industry needs.

The experience I gained in this institute not only broadened my mind but enhanced my analytical and problem-solving skills, and enabled me to build great relationships and networks globally. I had the privilege of being supervised by Professor John Ralston and Professor Jonas Addai-Mensah at UniSA. I was challenged intellectually by these two, which made the experience very enriching, and it also taught me to ask the right questions. I continue to attribute my success to these amazing professors.

John spent many years as Professor of Chemical Technology, and then decided that a new research institute was needed as part of the new University of South Australia. John had been The Wark's director from its inception until his retirement in 2012. John has received numerous awards and honours over the years, including: being made an Officer of the Order of Australia; South Australian of the Year; and South Australian Scientist of the Year. He is indeed a force for good global leadership in the science and academic field.

Jonas is very successful in his own right, having attracted huge funding and collaboration in Ghana. He is a chemical engineer by training and obtained his BEng (Hons) degree from University of Science and Technology, Ghana; his MSc from the Institute of Technology, Haifa, Israel; and his PhD from the University of Queensland, Brisbane. He has actively pursued research activities in the area of solid-liquid processing and separation, with applications to minerals, material and waste liquid processing and environmental cleaning.

Despite having great support from the Wark and my supervisors, there were still many changes I had to navigate as an international postgraduate STEM student. A postgraduate student is supposed to make an outstanding contribution to their subject. The Wark had a fairly good mix of international students of different genders, but it was still predominantly white male. The stereotype of the model PhD student was still evident. The lack of women in research and even in supervisors was evident across the universities at that time. There was a scarcity of women role models as they were outnumbered by males.

Over the years, this changed dramatically as the university was attracting more females. As I immersed myself into the new culture of research, a new country, and new environment, I started leaning in and seeking help from the few females we had. I was part of the P523 Australian Mineral Industries Research Association (AMIRA), which partly sponsored my studies. The P523 had ten sponsors in the project, which included global mining companies like BHP Billiton, Rio Tinto, Iluka Resources, Anglo Platinum, Cable Sands, Era Range Uranium Mine, Newcrest Mining, Outokumpu, Tiwest Joint Venture, and DeBeers. My scholarship covered both the tuition fees and the living expenses, including private health care and flights. This network was meant to solve problems for the mining industry. What The Wark would do was to combine all the mining companies' problems together.

The mining companies would subscribe and pay a fee to be part of this problem solving, in order to obtain the solution they sought. The Wark was well known for solving problems for the mining industry.

As usual, I was scheduled to have fortnightly meetings to discuss my progress with my supervisors. I spent more time with Professor Jonas as he was my principal. They explained the proposal and significance of the project and how my contribution was going to be in the bigger P523 project. I had to finalise my research problem and submit for approval to the University. The challenge was balancing the fundamental work, which was going to get me the PhD, and the application of the work in real plant problems.

There were sponsor meetings, where all the sponsors met at The Wark to get feedback on the work we were doing. This happened every six months. I started my PhD in April, and the next sponsor meeting was to be in July. In those three months, I had to produce something to present at the meeting. Sandy Lambert represented Anglo Platinum. All students who were working in the project had to present at the sponsor meeting. I was stressed. I had no idea what I was doing. This is where the *imposter syndrome* kicked in.

Adapting to new change can be a shock to your system. I initially struggled with adapting to my new environment. Firstly, I was still dealing with the loss of my father. Secondly, I had just gone through a divorce and was still coming to terms with being alone as a single mum. Thirdly, I had just moved to a new country, with a new culture. Fourth, I had left my son back in Africa and I was missing him. The other big change for me was doing a PhD, which in itself was a challenge. What made it even more challenging was the fact that I hadn't studied in a long time and, I was not very familiar with colloid chemistry. These were too many changes for me all at once. I was depressed.

I remember one day, I woke up and just cried. I asked myself what I had been thinking, coming to do a PhD. Who said I was smart in the first place? We had close to 70 students, both PhD and master's students, from all over the world—China, Japan, UK, France and Germany—there were many nationalities and they were all super smart. And every fortnight, three students were required to present at the seminar, in front of everyone, including research staff. Most of the time, Professor John Ralston and the other directors, Professor Roger Smart and Professor Roger Horn, would be there. Because some of the students were already presenting amazing results, I felt it made it even more difficult for me. Supervisors would be sitting there, asking intelligent questions. I felt exposed and stupid. I felt I was the dumbest person. As I sat in on one of the presentations, my internal voice said: *What was I thinking?... a girl from the township coming here overseas to be with smart people?* Professor Ralston and all the other supervisors were commenting that the presenter now had great publication material. My mother was right. 'You should have been a teacher or a nurse,' she would lament. Yes, my mother was right. *I'm not good enough, and this is not for me. I can't do this.*

The sponsor meetings were drawing closer. I still didn't have anything to show. I was losing confidence in my abilities. We had to do rehearsals with the project team. We were ten members in the P523 project, and this included research staff. We had a research assistant who was super smart, Le Huynh. She presented great results. I couldn't yet present any tangible results. I felt so stupid. I think they just felt sorry for me because they could tell I was nervous. Seeing my loss of confidence, my supervisors both encouraged me and provided some helpful guidance and advice on what I needed to work on. I didn't even know what they were talking about. But instead, I took notes. We were slowly approaching our sponsor meeting, which was three weeks away.

The day before the meeting, I decided not to read, and just watched television. I was exhausted and feeling depressed. In moments like those, I always seek the higher power. I kneeled and prayed, asking God, *What am I doing here? Why am I here? I need to go back home. I'm tired, I'm exhausted, and I don't want be here anymore. I miss my family; I miss my son. I just don't see any light at the end of the tunnel. I just want out. Please God.* I pleaded with God. The thought of the sponsor meeting the following day was just too much for me. I was stressed. Then, as I switched on the television, guess which program came up? *The Oprah Winfrey Show*. I thought, *I don't want to hear any motivation right now.*

As I was about to change channels, Oprah said (NOTE: These are not be the exact words but something along these lines), 'So when you quit, how is this going to serve you?' I thought, *This is bizarre… is she talking to me?* I paused but kept watching. 'So do you really think your situation is bad and you don't see any way out?' she continued to ask this woman.

'I'm tired, I'm depressed, and I just feel like nothing is working,' the woman replied.

Oprah continued to ask, 'Do you realise that someone, somewhere, wishes they have what you have? Have you reflected on the fact that all you need is within you right now?' I was hooked and increased the volume. Oprah went on and spoke about gratitude. She started relating her story of how she was once depressed and how she rose above her challenges.

I was astonished. *How did Oprah know I am going through this? It can only be divine intervention. Ask and it shall be given! Oprah is speaking to me.* It was an *aha* moment for me to realise how ungrateful I had become. Here I have a scholarship, and a company that's sponsoring me to do a PhD, with a guaranteed job after completing my studies. Does it get any better? They are paying for my son, for my living expenses, and I even have the airfares paid by this company, and yet I am about to give up because the PhD is hard and I feel like a fraud.

As I was thinking that I feel like a fraud, the same woman said something like, 'I feel like a fraud.' *What? Is she reading my mind?* I realised I was being selfish. I was being self-centred as I was so focussed on the mountain to climb and was comparing myself with others, which was not important. From that day onwards I started practising gratitude, because Oprah says when you have gratitude for life, it becomes even more abundant. It didn't mean that the challenge of the PhD was gone, but it meant that I started realising the possibilities of what I could be. I gave meaning to the wrong things. I had become obsessed with wanting to go back home. Oprah had long been my role model, and this was an epiphany moment for me.

Oprah asked the lady, 'Can you reflect on a time when you have been in a worse situation than right now, but you rose above the challenge?'

That night, I said a prayer to God for my forgiveness. How dare I be so ungrateful. The moment I shifted my perspective about my situation, and stopped focussing on the pain of losing my father but rather on the abundance in my life, the more I realised I had so much to give. As for the divorce, who hasn't divorced anyway? As for missing my son, many children don't even know their parents, let alone have a home. I started concentrating on the possibilities of what I could do for my son, for my family, for the company that trusted me, and for the many other people who depended on me. Who am I denying if I quit?

Then I knew what I needed to do. I started seeing possibilities. I started seeing how I had closed myself off from speaking to other people, from participating in some of the events, the social events, and connecting with other people. I had forgotten how to live my life. I was working from Sunday to Sunday, yet I was not making progress. I would go to the lab and just do experiments but not be strategic. I had no idea what I was doing. I realised there was so much I could do. I hadn't even travelled during weekends. Some of the students were exploring Adelaide like going to wineries etc. I had little money that I could use to explore inexpensive places during the weekend and connect with others. And the worst thing was, I was comparing myself with some of the research students who were experienced students and knew how to do research. I was being unfair to myself. This issue of the imposter syndrome is real.

I needed my brain to start doing other things. From that day, I shifted my perspective. I started making goals for myself: I was going to explore the things I've always wanted to do. I was going to connect with people that don't look like me. I was going to be curious and learn about other people's cultures. I wanted to know more about the Chinese, and I wanted to know more about the people from Iran. I wanted to know about the people from Russia. This is a multi-cultural, international institution with diverse students from all over the world.

There is an abundance, and I will make friends with people who don't look like me. In hindsight, I realised how we chose people who look like us, and we miss the opportunity to connect with others at a deeper level. I made a choice that day to step out of my comfort zone and connect with other students.

The next day, the sponsor meeting had finally arrived. I was not confident at all, but I felt much better than before. I was the second to present, and all I remember is mumbling some jargon that I didn't really understand well. I kept it short. I thought Anglo Platinum was going to pull out of the sponsorship after my presentation. I was so self-aware. Nonetheless, we had dinner in the evening, with Sandy and most people in the P523 project. He pulled me aside and said, 'Patience, well done.' I thought I didn't hear him well. *Well done for what?* I thought to myself. I was pleasantly surprised and shocked. I thought I did terribly. He went on without noticing my surprise, or maybe he pretended. He asked me, 'Is everything okay? Have you settled in well?' *Wow! This is not what I expected.*

That evening, the ice was broken. I was my happy self; we spoke, we laughed, and I felt much better. But I still felt like a fraud. *Let me enjoy this before the sponsor finally finds out that I am actually a fraud. When he finds out, they're just going to pull out that scholarship.* I just smiled, but I was forcing it because I was thinking I am not really what he thinks I am; I am simply not good enough.

At the meeting, the sponsors introduced themselves, and I noticed one African lady representing DeBeers. I kept wanting to speak to her but didn't get a chance until the next day. We connected immediately. Her name was Zandi. I was impressed and thought, *Wow, a black South African woman is the sponsor, and she flew from South Africa.* I was impressed with Anglo American. It was certainly a progressive company. I asked if she could join me for lunch, or if I could show her around if she was staying for a while. Indeed, she was going to be in Adelaide for an extra day as her flight was leaving the next day. I was happy. Her second sponsor meeting was finishing early, so we met up.

I was so happy to meet Zandi. She was my height, with a quiet persona, and very lovely. She was an engineer and super smart too. We first visited the thriving food and culture hub at the Adelaide Central Market. It was my favourite spot, with countless authentic eateries from Asia. We then jumped on a tram, and took just 20 minutes to one of my favourite city beaches, Glenelg. We were chatting about almost everything while walking. We had drinks at one of the bars and I asked her how she got to be where she was. She was humble and down to earth, downplaying her level in the organisation and she said that her boss had asked her to represent him as he was on leave.

Nonetheless, I was impressed with her. As we were chatting, she said something that struck me. I was so happy to have a sister in a foreign country. It was so refreshing and reminded me of home. She said, 'Patience, the work that you're doing is very important for us as a company… don't underestimate that.' I asked her how that was so, and if she could help me understand how my PhD was fitting into the bigger company problem.

Zandi explained to me how my work was solving a big problem for them. She said that as they were mining diamonds in one of their operations, they were encountering a swelling clay. Because of this swelling clay, when you add a chemical called a flocculant to help fine particles settle so that you can purify the water, the particles don't settle but instead swell even more and form a gel. That meant they then had to build even bigger tailings dams, which takes up more space and land—land that could be used for agriculture in communities. She said something else that struck a chord. 'Patience, do you know we need more land for communities?'

This was an epiphany moment for me. I realised my *why* for being here in Australia. I suddenly I knew I was doing something bigger, not just some fundamental work that goes to publication. I was now connected to my research project. I knew I was doing what I was supposed to do. I was solving a problem, not just for me but for communities. While I had some context, this additional information, which was so critical to really getting me up in the morning and finding meaning, made a huge difference. I had been asking myself: *Why did I sacrifice my easy life and my family to do a PhD in a foreign land?*

There is a model that is about finding something that you're passionate about, something where you're solving a problem, and something that you're good at, because finding meaning is about making a contribution. And when you feel that you're making a difference and having an impact, it makes it easier to get up in the morning. This talks to IKIGAI from the book by Hector and Miralles (2017. I had been on the brink of giving up. Zandi also said, 'Patience, I am so proud of you and the work you've done so far in this short space of time.' Talk about sisterhood! I thought, *What work? She has no idea I am a fraud.* We spent the whole wonderful day touring Adelaide, ending the day with a glass before she left. After that day, I knew what I was really problem-solving for. There have been studies undertaken about getting more women into STEM, especially young girls. The way we communicate to them, to encourage them, is super important. Girls want to know how it will help others. They need to connect to the STEM subject and the everyday life of helping others. We are nurturers.

It is said when people bring a positive energy into your space, somehow the universe brings more positive energy. There is power in surrounding yourself with the right people. When Zandi left the sponsor meeting that day, I was encouraged to do more. I started asking other people questions about their research. My research skills were not very good, and the way I was doing my literature review was a disaster. I then got a software that simplified my literature review.

A PhD student needs to be constantly reading and reviewing literature because it's constantly evolving. I became more resourceful. My academic English was not that great, and neither were my professional presentation skills. All these resources were made available to us at the university, but I never took the courses. From that day, I considered the list of courses I needed and I started attending, including excellent Powerpoint presentations, communication skills, Excel skills, and so on. I realised I wasn't reading enough as I was wallowing in my self-pity party, that voice: *I am new and not used to this culture.* It's like something just snapped out of me and fired me up.

When you join the university as a postgraduate student, you will be feeling successful and intelligent, with well-earned qualifications. I was selected among thousands of people and won the university scholarship. I had distinctions in most of my Honours degree chemistry subjects. However, I found that one starts to lose confidence and begin to question their own self-image. This often happens due to comparing oneself with other postgraduates who are further into their research. I was no different from most PhD students, but I was not networking or joining others for the after-work drinks or lunches to discuss challenges. I felt I didn't fit in. Even though they would invite me, I had lost my confidence and felt like a fraud. Everyone seemed smart and intelligent, except me.

The following day, Saturday, I decided to take massive action and write down things I'd wanted to do but had avoided. I had never wanted to participate in the wine tasting. I was going to try the wine. I planned to get out of my comfort zone. I would start talking to other people and ask for help. It was liberating. In that moment I started a new journey. The following Friday, with no clue about wine tasting, off I went. All I was doing was drinking wine. I wasn't tasting, but that didn't matter. I had no appreciation for the taste of wine, but it was a step forward for me to connect with other people. Although I was out of my comfort zone, I started getting to know other people.

The weeks went by… I was participating in the wine tasting, and joining others for lunch or drinks. I later decided to learn about wine and I booked for a wine tasting course and wine tour. It opened my eyes. That took my focus away from just a PhD, to being somebody who is more well-rounded and more creative. The wine tour was in the Barossa Valley and McLaren Vale. I became better and better at discerning wine, but most importantly, I started connecting informally with others. I started building relationships and I could easily speak with others and get to know them better, both students and supervisors.

Working towards a PhD is usually experienced as an isolating and lonely time especially when you live alone. Thank God, my son William and sister Zoe had joined me in my second year. Meeting other peer support groups helped a lot. The other important part was aligning my expectations with my supervisors who expected a certain degree of independence from me. I struggled initially. My writing skills were bad, and I could sense that they expected me to produce at least good quality written work, not just a draft. My drafts always came back with red ink all over. I thought Jonas was being brutal when he used to say, 'We can't give John this.' We would work on the draft, and maybe have at least five drafts; that's how bad I was.

When I felt I wasn't ready with any new insights, I started cancelling meetings with my supervisors. Not having regular meetings was a big mistake as it's easy to go off at a tangent. When I did have meetings, sometimes I wouldn't be honest with the challenges I was facing. I was too embarrassed and thought they would judge me. Talking to others helped a great deal, and learning to manage my supervisors was critical to my success.

Overcoming the Cultural Barriers of Being the Only One in the Room Who Looks Like Me

Many studies have been done on some of the differences between women and men in terms of leadership and succeeding in workplaces or even in business as entrepreneurs (Fels 2004, Helgesen and Goldsmith 2018, Sandberg 2013). Being self-critical is one barrier that most people can relate to. Men think they are brilliant most of the time, even if they don't meet half the criteria in a job interview. Fantastic women leaders, no matter how effective they've been or how much recognition they've received, often tend to focus on all the ways they believe they fall short. Successful women's tendencies to critique themselves instead of others opens them to different behavioural habits than men, who are more likely to accept recognition and deflect blame. This concept speaks to my background and my belief system that I am not good enough.

Working in a male-dominated environment, plus hearing your mum not believing you should be having a seat at the table, are challenging components, even though I knew my mum's advice was coming from a place of love and protection. My desire to be perfect stems from my mother, who I can say was a perfectionist. It took me a long time to realise that no one is perfect. Being compassionate about myself is one thing that took so long to master. When I did, I was free. I really don't have to be perfect. Besides, who set that standard and rule? Some rules we set for ourselves can be handicapping. Being authentic gave me permission to be myself.

Why confidence is important for success as a woman is a topic that has been debated and discussed globally (Hermina 2013, Helgesen and Goldsmith 2018, Sandberg 2013, Chamorro et al 2019). According to Harvard Business School Professor Cuddy (2012), projecting power is more about how you stand than how you talk. We did a power pose when I attended the global leadership Fellows Programme at Harvard, and I must say it definitely works. This is why I provide coaching sessions on building confidence as I realise how important it is. My logo has a power pose.

Confidence and courage are not qualities everyone can say they have. Why is it that only women need to show this character trait to be promoted? The imposter syndrome is an internal belief that you are not as good or competent as how others see you. It is a feeling that you are not deserving, worthy or capable of your current position. When we grow and expand our lives, occasionally we have a voice inside our head that doesn't really sound like our greatest supporting fan. It convinces us quite often that we are an imposter in our own life.

Showing confidence became an important part of my life, to ensure I reached the next level of success, especially given now I am an entrepreneur. I quickly understood that if I don't find a way to speak about the value of what I am doing, then I send a message that I don't put much value on it, and if I don't value it why should anyone else do so. I call this internal sales and marketing. As an entrepreneur, to sell yourself effectively, believing in what you have to offer is essential. This declaration initially made me uncomfortable so it may help to think in terms of why it mattered that I get ahead: What ultimately motivates me to reach the top? When I reflected on self-serving reasons, I turned that around to the knowledge that the world can benefit from my success. You must also learn to have confidence when dealing with rejection. I have been rejected several times. When someone or a company rejects you it's because they don't trust themselves to have you serve them. Failure is not the opposite of success. Failure is a mechanism for learning.

This creates a big impact on your performance and results, because it means that you will self-sabotage. You won't project confidence; you won't be an effective leader, because people can sense your lack of belief; your business won't take off because you will be procrastinating... the list goes on. But more than just the results, the imposter syndrome affects your well-being, happiness and self-worth. It simply doesn't feel good to be stuck second-guessing yourself at every turn. What made it worse for me was when I was seeing others succeed.

Confidence is one characteristic that I didn't necessarily have when I was growing up. We grew up in a township, and my mum used to cut our hair to bald until we finished primary school. We never wore fancy clothes, we sewed and made our own. Some of our relatives had a different upbringing than us—they had the freedom to wear anything, or could plait their hair. Not in my mother's house. We were like the underdogs. I learned to be confident. When I spoke to one Chinese guy at The Wark, his English was not that good, but he was utterly confident about his work, as though he had done it before. I thought to myself, *Hang on, he is still trying to speak and present his results in English, and here I am complaining.* Even though I felt better over time, I didn't immediately stop feeling like an imposter sometimes. Getting a PhD is not an easy experience.

When you surround yourself with positive people, positive things seem to happen. It's an energy. After the day I had spoken with Zandi, I went to the library. As I was doing my literature review, I found a paper that I had not seen anywhere before. It discussed one particular flocculent that had been tried by the US bureau of mines, which worked well for clay minerals a long time ago: polyethylene. I read this paper and I started getting even more papers that I had never seen. As I read and analysed, I realised there was a gap in the knowledge of something that hadn't been explored before. The penny dropped... it made sense to me.

I quickly designed my experiments as I knew what I was looking for. I had a hypothesis surrounding two types of clay minerals and how they behaved in different process waters. I worked day and night on my experiments. In less than a month, I had phenomenal results. The more I asked myself intelligent questions and then researched more, I realised there was a gap in the knowledge regarding these clays. Both types of clays were dominant for most of the sponsors' mining tailings. I was excited, and suddenly my confidence started growing. I was happier, but I didn't tell my supervisors as it felt too premature. I repeated the experiments, emulating the process conditions in the mine processing plants several times. I started designing even more sophisticated experiments using certain techniques to confirm what I found. It was confirmed.

Finally, I got it. I put together my presentation for our next meeting, when I was ready to share with my supervisors. They were impressed. I was proud of myself. I started focussing on this particular flocculant and comparing it with the traditional one commonly used to treat these difficult minerals. It was a breakthrough for me. The power of talking to the right people with the right energy cannot be underestimated.

In 2001, I received a CSIRO award for best presentation poster at the National Australian Colloids and Surface Science Student Conference. When it came to winning awards, there was still a nagging feeling of not feeling worthy of the praise for my accomplishments. I didn't think I was worthy or deserving of recognition. Despite being a high achiever, I felt it was only a matter of time until it was found out that I really was an imposter with limited skills or abilities. At this conference, big Australian universities converge to discuss the latest research findings. What made it even more special was that students presented, and there were two awards given to the best poster presentation and the best oral presentation. There was some kind of competition, especially with Melbourne University Syrsity.

On the other hand, even though I was happier as I had found interesting results and was ready to present at any conference, as a mother, I was trying to juggle studies and spending time with my son. My weekends were spent taking him to sports. He loved every single sport offered in Australia, from skating, cricket, Aussie footy, soccer, tennis, swimming… everything. I had no life outside my son's activities during the week and weekends. I was literally either doing my work or I was with my son at his sports events. Then those days of going out stopped. I read books and sometimes I would watch comedies or go to the movies with my son and my sister. I never missed the wine tasting weekends. Sometimes we would travel around Adelaide when there were no sports. Because of my hectic personal schedules, I was going to present a poster presentation for the conference.

This conference was held in McLaren Vale. I now had made friends and I was feeling more like myself. We all did our presentations, and on the last day of the conference, the winners for the best poster and the best presenter were to be announced. As we were sitting there waiting to hear who the winner was for the poster presentation, I hadn't been thinking it could be me, in fact, I was in the bathroom when the announcement was made. As I entered the conference room, people started clapping. I was shocked. I had just won the award for the best poster presentation. There was also a monetary reward: I think it was $500. That was a breakthrough for me, and I cried with joy—not because of the award but what it represented: the impact of the research.

As usual, there was lots of wine and dancing as we celebrated. I was always the first to dance. Put on music if you want to see an African have fun. I was happy but still had a nagging feeling: I still thought I was a fraud. I even confided in my mate, Val. I thought others felt sorry for me as an African woman. Everyone was congratulating me, but I was embarrassed. 'It's nothing; I was lucky,' I kept saying.

Towards the end of that same year, I won The Wark best PhD research student presenter. I won the award based on innovation and the scientific value in strong technological importance, which was voted by the top professors at the institute. I was proud of myself. Finally, this had given me an endorsement that I am enough. I had unleashed my superpowers. That day when Oprah said, 'You are enough,' I thought, *Yes, I am enough.* When we had the sponsor meeting in subsequent years, I could stand with my head held high, because I knew what I was all about.

I learned quickly that to succeed, you needed to publish early on. I was pretty late in getting my paper out. Firstly, my English was not up to scratch. I decided to enrol for a professional English writing course. Most of my fellow students had already started publishing. I was way behind, but that didn't matter. I worked harder and by the end of the second year, I had written three papers. I still had self-doubt. The issue now was not that I felt like a fraud any longer, but there was something deep and profound about my limiting belief systems. My sisters always appeared effortlessly confident and, with time, I learned from them to fake confidence. I started challenging my assumptions of not being good enough and that I was constantly headed for failure. The book that transformed my thinking was *Mind Power* by Kohoe (2001).

My favourite place had become a book shop. I loved going there. I would pick over five books a day, included among them was *Rich Dad Poor Dad* by Kiyosaki (1997). Since my coaching days, I know many of my clients who could achieve so much more if they believed in themselves. I have actually found that mostly its women who doubt themselves, more so than men. *Mind Power* and the book *The Secret* all talk about how your thoughts can shape your future. Mostly, you are what you think you are. It took me many years to get to that point.

I started writing and publishing, and as I got more papers out, I was then publishing one after the other. The more I did experiments, and then designed new experiments and asking new questions, the more I got a new body of knowledge. It started getting easier and better. I started helping others who were new PhD, honours or exchange students. I even started working in the labs helping honours chemistry students with their experiments. I eventually published six papers in peer reviewed journals, and my work was applied to real plant work that was carried out.

My experience at this multidisciplinary institute, which is internationally recognised for solving complex industry problems, enhanced my problem-solving skills. I finished my PhD. Completing the writing process was much easier because I had already published. I was working hard writing and/or reading literature reviews, and sometimes sleeping five hours. I never stopped writing. My supervisors rewarded me with two international conferences to present in both Brazil and in Cape Town.

The conference in Brazil was the 11th International Conference on Colloid and Surface Science, held in August 2003, in Iguassu Falls. The other one in Cape Town was held in September 2003. It was the XXII International Mineral Processing Congress, held for the first time in Africa. These were big conferences. I submitted my papers and both were accepted. I was ecstatic. What made it even more special was that by the time I attended the conferences, I would have submitted my PhD thesis, so these opportunities felt like rewards.

I am forever grateful for the support of my supervisors and from others within The Wark. I don't think I could have completed my studies without their support. This experience not only helped me to think strategically and creatively, but most importantly, I built amazing networks and relationships. It was one of the best experiences in my entire life and I'm grateful for the opportunity that was given to me. Knowing that I was supported and had sponsors from a global mining company always sits in my heart.

I reflected as I was packing my bags to leave Australia. It was again that time to say goodbye. I was filled with gratitude, and with so much love for the place that gave me the opportunity to learn, to be challenged, and to connect with smart, like-minded people. I learned what it is to connect with people who don't look like you. I learned how to lean in. I was filled with an appreciation of a wonderful experience. I remember when I was struggling one time with my PhD, and my son was only five years old. I was complaining about how hard balancing the work was, and he said, 'Mum, you are strong like Superman,' and as a single parent, all I could think of in response was, *How can I be better daily and how can I add value?*

The three-and-a-half years I spent in Australia not only broadened my mind, but I built great relationships globally. The sponsorship from the mining companies goes a long way for me to always remember that *I am* because somebody said lets nurture and grow a talented black woman, and make a difference. I will always advocate for the industry and be their brand ambassador, as I believe so much can still be done. As I was packing, I reminisced about the great network of people that I had connected with during my stay in Australia: from Germany, Australia, the UK, Sweden, France, Iran, India, China, and more. The one who stood out was my friend, Val. She was a Scottish lady and crazy like me. We would dance like nobody was looking. I remember when we were at a particular conference, we were always the ones to participate in karaoke. We would have so much fun. I was whatever I wanted to be at those times… I was in my happy moments. We would sing, and I'm not a good singer, but somehow people just loved it, or so I thought. Scot meets African queen. Those were the days in Australia.

Then there was Veronique, the exchange student from France, who taught me how to make *Charlotte*, a delicious French cake. I tried to learn French, and her English was not so good, so we agreed that we would teach each other. As life happened, we kept in touch, and when I went to Europe in 2015, I visited her and her family in Lyon. I have not seen Val since then and I don't know where she is. I've kept in touch with some of the Australian friends like Associate Professor Gayle Morris and Professor Kate Fox, who also participated in my Legacy Project. I am a firm believer of being connected to people and making an impact.

Work hard and play hard was our mantra. The year before I left, we had a big Christmas party. I was on the organising committee and the theme was retro. What an experience: we had a blast. Dancing and wearing wigs was so much fun. As I reflected on when I started, compared to when I was leaving, it showed me how life can change for the better when you don't give up and you focus on gratitude— when you connect with people, when you open your heart and mind and think differently, when you look at life from a point of gratitude—

but most importantly, when you know what you're doing is solving big problems and making an impact to create a better world than the one you found.

Patience graduating from University of South Australia
with a PhD in Mineral Processing

* * *

And then my journey back to where I came from…

Brazil is the largest country in both South America and Latin America, with over 211 million people. It is the world's fifth-largest country by area, and the sixth most populous. Its capital is Brasília, and its most populous city is São Paulo. The main spoken language is Portuguese. Brazil is the second largest global iron ore exporter, and produces copper, gold, aluminium bauxite (one of the five biggest producers in the world), manganese (one of the five biggest producers in the world), tin (one of the biggest producers in the world), niobium (concentrates 98% of the known niobium reserves in the world), and nickel. It is the world's largest producer of amethyst, topaz and agate, and is a big producer of tourmaline, emerald, aquamarine and opal (Wikipedia Brazil).

Brazil has many tourist attractions, including famous places like the Amazon, the famous Carnival and the Cristo Redentor Carcavado. The International Colloids and Surfaces Science Conference that I was invited to speak at was taking place at another famous tourist attraction, the Iguassu Falls. The Iguaçu River drops spectacularly in a semicircle of 247 waterfalls that thunder down into the gorge below, at the point where Brazil, Paraguay, and Argentina meet, just above the falls. Protected by the UNESCO-acclaimed Iguaçu National Park, the falls are spectacular.

I landed in São Paulo, Brazil, and we were directed to the usual immigration and customs, which was a very interesting experience. I collected my bags and had all my documentation, including my visa and everything that I needed to pass through immigration. I was the only black female on that flight. I was singled out to go through a thorough security check. I remained calm and allowed the process to take place. I was eventually allowed to pass through but after a lot of interrogation. I arrived in Sao Paulo and spent time exploring the city before travelling to Iguassu Falls for the conference.

My colleagues were arriving on different dates whereas I had arrived a week before the conference to explore Brazil. I was happy that I was presenting on the second day of the five-day conference. I couldn't sleep because I was presenting in front of more than 500 people. I spent the whole day practising when other people were having fun. The day arrived when I had to present. I did well and was happy with myself. All those fears that I had before were just a waste of time. We visited the phenomenal Iguassu Falls and then my trip was cut short as I had to go back to South Africa where my job was waiting for me.

At the age of 32, I had obtained my PhD in Minerals and Material Sciences, with my thesis titled, *Surface chemistry and improved dewatering of clay dispersions*. I had published in more than ten papers in peer-reviewed journals and had presented at international and national conferences, however, despite this professional success, the experience was not all smooth sailing. Completing a PhD research degree enabled me to learn to challenge conventional wisdom or accepted thinking, and required a highly motivated, independent and resilient person. The Wark enhanced my resourcefulness, interpersonal skills and confidence due to the opportunities offered to work alongside some of the world's best researchers. I will forever be grateful.

Exercise

Most people see reality as something that exists in its physical form, rather than something they are responsible for creating through mind focus. The truth is that individuals exercise choice and can shape reality. By force of will, you can decide to be happy. By controlling your thoughts, you can exert influence on the conditions around you, recognising that life does not have to be hard. With the right perspective, life can seem easy and enjoyable—attitude is up to you. The thoughts you have can actually exert energy towards the world around you. You can learn to manipulate your thoughts, choosing which ones to accept and which to reject, in order to shape reality to your will (Kehoe 2001).

The situations you find yourself in often are manifestations from inside your mind and you are responsible for how your inner self affects the outer world (Bryne 2006). Your actions define your nature, and so your nature is also malleable to your will. You define yourself, so positive affirmations have positive impacts. In this world where the thoughts and nature of the individual are in constant interplay with external reality, a *law of attraction* is at work. Both the things you love and the things you hate will be drawn to you because you focus on them.

Therefore, it is important to be very mindful of what you choose to focus on, as the concepts and thoughts you entertain will become part of your reality. This gives you the power to influence your circumstances positively, simply by using your mind. By positively controlling your thoughts, you can achieve goals by fully imagining success. Build your self-esteem by focussing on the positive. Control the beliefs that dictate your behaviour.

Many studies have shown that being thankful can have many positive health benefits. For example, practicing gratitude can lead to more intimate and connected relationships, less depression, more motivation and engagement, and better overall mental well-being. I remember at Harvard, we were asked to write gratitude letters to our loved ones after learning about the positive effects of gratitude. How often do we express gratitude in our lives? If it improves our lives, our health, and makes us happy, why don't we practise gratitude as a daily ritual instead of complaining? A positive approach opens many doors for more positive things to come into our lives.

I practise gratitude daily in the morning by meditating on the three things I am grateful for each day.

1. Daily, think of three things you are grateful for in your life. It might be anything from having food on your table or having a great friend, to having a job that pays your bills.
2. Make it your daily practice for five minutes for a month, first thing in the morning. Journal how you feel by the end of the day.

Request a pre-order for a gratitude journal filled with inspirational quotes from our upcoming e-store launching soon.

www.unleashingmysuperpowers.com/estore

CHAPTER 4

WHO IS MY MENTOR AND SPONSOR?

Don't look for the light at the end of the tunnel. It's not there.
You are the light. It has been inside of you all along.
– Xo Iva Xo

The issue of unconscious bias in the workplace is an aspect that is still not fully explored, especially with regard to closing the gender gap, and needs further work from both men and women.

In 2015, the movie *Hidden Figures* was released. I watched it and I must say, it brought back some of the memories of being in a room where you are the only one who looks like you. The movie is about Katherine Johnson, who died at age 101, and how she overcame American racial segregation and sexism stereotypes in science (NASA). Ultimately, the movie reflects on the importance of determination, hard work and resilience with the message that women can be anything they want to be. They can unleash their superpowers to succeed despite obstacles. She was one of a group of the finest mathematical minds in the country, who calculated the precise trajectories that would facilitate the Apollo 11 moon-landing in 1969.

She is a well celebrated woman of colour in STEM. There are many others who have contributed to the STEM professions, but Mrs Johnson stands out for me. She faced many challenges of gender discrimination and racism but against all odds, she achieved. Hers is truly an inspirational story, one that moved me to tears. I realised how much we have now progressed in male-dominated workplaces, but the challenges have reincarnated in a different form. The barriers are invisible, which makes it worse because you can't put a hand on it. Government, companies and many institutions have put in place policies and procedures to deal with issues of gender diversity, inclusion and equality, but there is nothing to deal with subtle, invisible, discriminatory sexist behaviours.

Katherine Johnson's story sounds and feels familiar, and it happened almost a century ago. We are entering the twenty-first century and yet women especially still feel discrimination. We completed a survey of 100 women working in male-dominated (STEM) workplaces, and the majority felt they don't belong and that the barriers are invisible. Being the only woman and being a black woman makes it even worse. When a woman is assertive and uses her voice, it's deemed aggressive and difficult. When she is confident, that's arrogance.

The behaviours that show gender discrimination include the fact that women feel being assertive is a trait that is not lauded. While men exhibit it, they condemn it in women as Sandberg (2013) says in her book. Being lonely, especially in leadership positions, is common. Women lack other women in male-dominated workplaces with whom they can discuss the challenges they face as a woman, and through whom they could seek guidance. This is where having a coach and a mentor helps. There are many instances where I was the only black woman, surrounded by white males. This is why we need more women in leadership positions.

Unconscious bias is real and is one of the major barriers to women's advancement in STEM professions. Women have been campaigning to have a seat at the table for many years, but the progress is very slow, especially in leadership positions in the mining industry. Throughout my career, I have been the only woman, and regularly, the only black one. What makes it worse is having to prove myself and my capabilities, despite my experience. This was highlighted to me once when a male counterpart, with less experience and not having gone through the same challenges, was promoted faster. Sometimes, no matter how good your work is, it gets extra scrutiny, including in discussion or decision-making. I have experienced the PhD (Pull Her Down) syndrome: the curse of being an educated, young black female.

Women can also be their own worst enemies. One of the stereotypic behaviours is agism. Women love to address other women in professional settings, using derogatory titles such as *my dear, my love, sweetie,* or *darling.* How can we be taken seriously when we address each other as we address our children in professional settings? This is an age issue. The first conversation some women have with me when I meet them is, 'Oh darling, you look so young.' That's what I have experienced most of my life. Again, we are putting emphasis on looks.

Historically, maintaining youthfulness was desirable to keep your man. It was not meant for yourself but for the men, as they tended to prefer younger women to marry, giving rise to polygamy. I used to feel embarrassed, especially when it came from people I respected. We are accentuating the issue of making our young girls feel as though growing old is bad or a curse. We need to embrace aging gracefully because we are spiritual beings and we all age differently. Looks dissipate, and what remains is your soul and your impact in the world.

I often get asked how I navigated these barriers to achieve as a black woman in STEM, from being a metallurgist, to being vice president of a global mining company. This is why I have written this book. I have faced many barriers, some unconscious and others simply stereotyping from males. How I navigated took a lot of grit, self-confidence and self-belief, and support from great relationships, but most importantly, knowing when to move.

Relational Skills That No One Teaches You (Why EQ is More Important Than Ever)

I returned to South Africa with a job waiting for me in the mineral processing division. I was excited to be back and to put my four years of studying into important use. I was ready to solve any mineral processing challenges with all I knew. So much had changed: the economy was booming; the rand was at its highest strength but this was hurting the mining industry. I quickly bought myself a house and got my son settled at a nearby local school. Johannesburg was booming with housing developments. There were shopping centres being built left, right and centre in the Sunninghill area where I lived. I was happy.

I had to adapt to a new culture again after having been overseas for close to four years in the safe and protected environment of being a PhD research student in Australia. The biggest challenge was to adapt to the male-dominated workplace culture of mining, and how things were being done in our department of mineral processing. My first few weeks were spent in familiarising myself with how the mining operations work, and mostly about meeting people.

Have you ever felt as though you are being ignored and misunderstood? You want your point to be heard, and you yearn to be heard, but no one is listening? When you disagree but everyone seems to agree, you feel like you are being fake. It took me a long time to understand politics. That is why, historically, in the mining industry, safety statistics used to be bad, because no one felt free to speak up. This was the old way and, yes, things have changed since then. You don't want to be seen as the odd one who is always raising issues or having a different viewpoint. I was always the odd one.

Settling in at the research centre took a while for me. The style of leadership was different. I had been nurtured, supported and challenged, and here I was, with routine work that offered little challenge. I could do many flotation tests daily, with my eyes closed— a job any person with a bit of training can do; in my view, it was wasted talent. My other colleagues had very cushy, nice, challenging fundamental projects that had a visible impact. Four months into the role, I needed to speak with my manager. I felt underutilised and wanted more. I was tired of routine work and wanted challenging projects.

My manager was a very nice guy, but we had different working styles and approaches to solving problems. He was laid back and comfortable with his routine work and his nice team, who were also comfortable with how things were working. I wasn't. I took the courage to bring my concern to him. I was not very tactful. I said it like it was: 'This work is not challenging enough for me and I feel underutilised. Can I propose some projects or be given challenging projects?' I thought I was being true to myself and being honest. The meeting didn't go well when I raised the issue. Nonetheless, I had raised my concern and I wanted change. I didn't back down. The meeting ended with me feeling I didn't belong. I was frustrated. I was like a square trying to fit in a circle. He felt challenged, which was not my intention. He had built his entire career over 20 years doing what he loved, the same way, and dedicated his life to serving the organisation, and here I was coming to tell him, 'Let's change the way you have been doing your work.' How dare I!

In hindsight, I think he didn't know what to do with me. Eventually, he gave in and gave me one challenging big project that was new. The next day, he called me for a meeting to have a conversation. He said he had considered my request. He would allow me to take over one of the water projects and solve one other problem that had been brought to him, on a non-floating ore in one of the new operations in the northern part of the country, and another on water quality issues. My manager also mentioned that for the operations people to co-operate, I had to go to the operations to better understand. They knew I didn't like going to the mining processing operations, and this project meant I probably had to go to the operations on a weekly basis. I was happy. I thought it was easy, until I started the job. Little did I know it was going to be one of the most challenging tasks ever.

Firstly, this job meant no more staying in nice offices with comfortable air conditioners. Secondly, I had to drive to the operations to investigate, speak to the plant managers and get samples, and then do the test work in the lab. I was given a team to work with and we had to solve some problems, from non-floating ore to water challenges that were impacting the operations. Not only that, but I also had to be in Rustenburg, a two-hour drive from Johannesburg, for pilot plat trials. I had asked for a challenging project and it didn't come in a nice package as I expected. I took the challenge.

I immediately thought about my son and how I would manage. I was a single mother; my son had just started at a new school and was trying to adjust, and I had to collect him after school. I could see that juggling travelling to operations and driving back on time to pick him up was going to be challenging. I had no one else except my sister, Diana but she was doing her master's degree at the University of Witwatersrand and she occasionally arrived home late. I had two choices: either Diana would have to cut short her studies in the afternoons when I couldn't make it back in time, or I would have to get a taxi to pick up my son. That would be difficult and expensive, so I could see I had to find a plan.

I would drive alone for four to six hours, far away to remote operations in the north-west and north of Johannesburg, where most of the company operations are situated. This is called the platinum belt. At first, this new role was difficult. I had to drive to the operations. Then change into the plant overalls, do safety training and get security clearance. I couldn't do it all in a day. I had to sleep overnight sometimes and then do the work in the morning. It was onerous. I missed my routine lab work. All of a sudden, that routine work I so hated seemed like the best job ever. I planned my trips. Failure was not a choice for me. What would Peter or Sandy say? How about my professors back in Australia? I really needed to do this.

Knowing your client is one of the most important things in business. The same applies internally in an organisation. The operations guys were mostly interested in cost reduction, increasing efficiency and improving recovery or safety, as those were their KPIs. I quickly learned the hard way that if you come with any fundamental research that is far-fetched, you will get a backlash. For the one project of improving recoveries by testing various reagents, I started with Rustenburg operations where I was lucky as the plant superintendent, Silas Mokoele, was a male who looked like me. He was such a great person: accommodating and helpful. He took me through the 101-culture of how things worked there. He told me not to mention words like *fundamental studies*. He explained that all they wanted to know was how I would help reduce costs, make the operations more efficient, and increase recovery, but most importantly, to do it safely. It was safe, profitable platinum.

I now grasped how things could be done. I would drive for two to six hours, deep into the mine operations, listening to my favourite music by Angelique Kidjo, Miriam Makeba or Yvonne Chaka. There was something soothing about listening to this music. Miriam Makeba is a well-known musician and she grew to fame with the song, *Patapata*. Yvonne Chaka Chaka's *Umqombothi*, and Brenda Fassie's *Vulindlela*, were comforting. I then went to Amandelbult operations, where I met another amazing *brother*. Anglo Platinum was progressive in regard to advancing and promoting black South Africans. This man helped me and we could talk easily.

Then I met another brother at the Union Operations. There was only one plant manager woman that I met. I was impressed with her and so inspired that a female was working in the operations that it reinforced my knowledge that *I can do this*. The power of having role models should not be underestimated! Had it not been for my son still in primary school, I could have moved to operations. I worked with the supply chain teams in trying to get an alternative source to perform trials on the other new reagents. This quickly opened many doors in working with a multidisciplinary team, and my problem-solving role was beginning to get exciting. I started enjoying the plant visits with a view to solving their problems.

Taking over these challenging projects turned out to be the best decision ever as I learned a lot in regard to the processing operations. Most importantly, I built a huge network that became valuable in my later career. One of the things I soon grasped was that the mining industry appreciates someone who has done their part in mining operations. If you are a woman in STEM, getting your hands dirty is part of the game. There is no shortcut to success. Although you are in corporate, just understanding the real operational challenges makes you credible. I am, to this day, very grateful for that decision. It may not have sounded like it, but that boss did me a great favour. However, the inclusion we are advocating for is about how organisations should create flexibility for mothers. Imagine if I didn't have my sister and live-in helper. These are real challenges women are facing and navigating. The good news, as you will read in later chapters, is that in this 21st century, we are now leveraging technology to build the smart mines of the future, which will be a great competitive advantage for a company that leads in this space to help more women.

The role of mentors cannot be emphasised enough. Studies have shown how having a mentor helps you to navigate and succeed in your career. I was now settling into my new role, spending more time in the operations and starting to enjoy it. Peter, always checked on me, primarily because, I suppose, the company had invested a lot, and they also wanted to ensure I was settling in well. Having a male champion supporting you is one of the greatest things that male-dominated workplaces should do. I was fortunate to have that support from my sponsors when I did my PhD. When I returned to South Africa, they still had an open-door policy. The question Peter would always ask was, 'Are you okay, Patience?' That was enough for me, as this showed some caring, and I knew I had someone I could talk to should I need any help.

I was now enjoying my visits to these operations sites. That was where I understood everything. I had been visiting all the concentrating processing operations for Anglo Platinum; I now knew them well. It was while I was working on the talc depressant project that I was nominated for a leadership development program: The Anglo Achievers Program. It was for high-potential, mid-career professionals across Anglo American. There were three from Anglo Platinum. The others were from Anglo Base, Anglo Gold, Mondi, Head office and Anglo Coal—a total of 30. The program was a four-week program spread over six months. It was an eye opener for me and extremely impactful.

The power of developing talented people is phenomenal, and I can never fault this company for their care and development of its employees. Leaders being deliberate about developing their people is critical. This program changed my perceptions about career choices, in understanding leading oneself, and in understanding the crucial drivers of profitability for a mining company. There were great facilitators and coaches, and I later met one of them when she came to help with culture change in another organisation where I worked.

We learned about the power of personal mastery, understanding Anglo American strategy and how everything fits. We had various speakers, and one who stood out was Mr Ben Magara, the general manager of one of the coal operations. He was passionate about safety. It was a transformational program that certainly improved my leadership skills, especially in the field of emotional intelligence. Of crucial importance was understanding yourself and your career aspirations, and taking charge to ensure you achieved your goals.

We had to set up SMART goals for ourselves for a minimum of three years to achieve them. I knew exactly what I wanted after I asked the questions: *As a woman in a STEM career, how do I rise to a leadership position if I don't have commercial experience? What was the leadership pipeline for a specialist in STEM, to rise to a leadership role?* It was clear that having business acumen was the only way for me to get to where I wanted to be. I drew up my clear goals with specific action plans on what *good* looked like for my career. I was going to complete my benchmarking exercises on the water quality of the operations to get best practice and solve this problem for the company. Then I would do a Management Development Program (MDP) and finally move into strategy so that I could develop my business acumen, and then eventually get to the general management level. That was the plan I presented to the team. I visualised myself in strategy.

We had to take the plan and execute. I did just that. With my plan, I immediately approached my boss and requested to be selected for the MDP, so that I could learn the commercial, strategy, and financial aspects of the business. One of my strengths is problem solving, as my brain was wired to solve problems, but I had no understanding of the commercial implications and how things fit together. I had no idea about cost optimisation. I could solve the problem with a new reagent, but the problem was that it may not be a viable business case, and that's where I needed to understand what was meant by *a business case*. Initially, my boss pushed back and said I was still learning the operations and that this would be a distraction, but I convinced him and after a long back and forth convincing, he eventually gave in and agreed.

I was selected for the MDP. It was in-house but led by Wits Business School (WBS). There were more than 80 delegates selected from all over the company, which probably at that time had more than 100,000 employees. These included senior managers from the different parts of the organisation and there were perhaps three women, with the rest predominantly white males. They lectured fortnightly, within the company premises at the Rustenburg training centre. We would spend a week learning a module and it was intensive.

My life was now so interesting, and I was happy. My career was beginning to take off: I had a strong network internally, and life was getting better. I was solving operational problems that was going to make an impact. I was now the go-to person for something valuable: solving water challenges and flotation problems, optimisation for concentrate operations. My boss and I now had a better working relationship, and this included my mates and my team. I was generally happy; except I was still struggling to balance taking care of my son with my trips to the mine processing operations.

Change is inevitable. In early 2004, the organisation restructured, with a merger between two business units, the research centres, as they felt there was an unnecessary duplication of work. The industry was hurting due to a strong South African rand. Anglo American Research and the Anglo Platinum Research Centre were to merge to become one: Anglo Research. It meant many changes, including relocating offices. Emotions were high and there was a lot of uncertainty.

As part of the Phase-1 process, I was asked if I could move to Anglo Research, which was part of the bigger Anglo-American group. In retrospect, this seemed like a great move; it not only gave me an opportunity to meet more people, but it enabled me to be truly global. I reflected on my career goals and realised this might be an opportunity for me to learn other commodities. I became excited at the many possible opportunities. What if I extend the water optimisation benchmarking project to all other operations at Anglo American? I went to speak with Peter. I told him he may consider moving me to Anglo Research so that I could start working on other operations. That happened fast, but unfortunately, I had to work on only the Anglo-American operations first, as the merging was going to take place. I was then moved to Anglo Research. I was the only one who made the move at that time.

A new beginning with a new boss started. I was asked to present on the work I had done so far, to the divisional directors at Anglo American, at which the executives, Pat Lowrey and Paul Dempsey sat. My life was going to change from that day. I was given the water project to benchmark across all operations. As a woman in mining, having access and visibility to the decision makers created a space for me to thrive. Not only was my talent recognised, but I could now use all my skills to make a difference. I was not denied an opportunity as a woman—or as a black woman. What was important was asking for what I wanted, asking for help, and also being clear on my career goals. If you wait for life to happen, life can take you anywhere. As I reflect on some of the breakthrough or epiphany moments, I see that I had to be the driver: to make things happen. I had the courage to ask but also knew what I wanted. This was now the beginning of a journey into the global space of Anglo American.

Trip to Chile: Breaking Barriers of a Male-Dominated Industry as a Young Mother

Working in the mining industry was not something that I had earlier visualised. It's an industry where you can easily have a love-hate relationship: love it for its rich culture and abundant opportunities, but hate it for some of the barriers that may exist for women to enter and to progress. My experience at Anglo Research made me realise that some of the barriers to women's promotion was the inability to work in remote places. This makes male counterparts take on more challenging, high visibility projects, where they can be seen and get an opportunity to be promoted. This is especially true for jobs that need physical strength, like a rock driller in the mining industry.

As for the overalls that we wore when working in the mining operations, firstly, as they were not designed for women, you can look like some freaky humpty-dumpty. Those overalls were meant for males, so most of the time you will find that the waist is perfect, but the hip area is very tight or doesn't fit at all, especially for those of us women who have been gifted in that area. The other interesting thing is the shoes, which were always big. I never had the right size, even when I requested the smallest available. We are females and we want to look good and not weird and funny. These are some of the things that may have changed over time, but in those days, you had to make do with those large-waisted overalls that were tight on the hips and made you feel self-conscious. Maternity wear overalls were never heard of either.

My colleague Robert and I were going to work together on this massive project, and we had a plan to execute it across different continents and countries. The first part of the trip was the South American mining operations.

This necessitated a trip to Chile where we were to visit at least three processing operations. Our itinerary was ready, with flights booked and accommodation all sorted. I had been looking forward to this trip and while at the airport, I went to a bookshop to buy a booklet that translates English to Spanish. On the plane we were allocated seats in separate aisles. I was sitting with an middle aged, white male, probably in his early 50s. I was in my early thirties but probably looked to him as though I was in my early twenties. He just looked at me and smiled. I am sure he was wondering, 'what is this young girl doing flying to Santiago?' I was in my comfortable sneakers and trackpants. I couldn't be bothered to look businesslike in the business class, which made it even worse as I looked like some 21-year-old with my small stature.

We didn't talk much, but when we were about to land, we started chatting. I am sure he was burning to ask me the question, as I was probably the only female, and black, in that business class. 'My name's Mike; what's yours?' I politely responded with a smile, as I knew what his next question was going to be. 'So, what's taking you to Santiago? Do you have family?'

I replied, 'No, it's work.'

'Wow,' he exclaimed. 'May I ask which company?'

'Anglo American.'

He was clearly stunned. 'You work in the mines?'

'Yes.'

'That company is very progressive, I must say,' he replied. I nodded, agreeing with him. He was clearly impressed. Then we started chatting about the work I do. He had his own company based in Santiago. We spoke about many things and I actually enjoyed having a chat with him. The barriers were down. It was like chatting with a colleague.

Flying to Chile took me into an entirely different world. Chile is a country in western South America with a population of more than 17.5 million. It occupies a long, narrow strip of land between the Andes to the east and the Pacific Ocean to the west. The capital and largest city is Santiago and the national language is Spanish. Chile hosts some of the largest mines in the world and is rich in mineral resources, especially copper and lithium.

The first mine we visited was the large Collahuasi copper mine, located in northern Chile, about 180 kilometres southeast of the port of Iquique, at an altitude of 4,400 metres. Collahuasi represents one of the largest copper reserves in Chile and in the world, having estimated reserves of 3.93 billion tonnes of copper. We took a flight to Iquique from Santiago where we spent a night. We had a car and driver waiting for us to drive us up north to Collahuasi mine. I never made it to the mine. We had been warned about the possible effects of high altitude, where most of the operations are in Chile. I slept in the car while on the way to Collahusi. As we were a few kilometres from the operation, I woke up feeling sick. I couldn't breathe and I started throwing up. I didn't know that altitude would so affect me. Fortunately, they anticipate these kinds of reactions from people and there are mobile clinics along the way. I was immediately conveyed to a nearby clinic on a stretcher and was given an oxygen mask to assist my breathing.

* * *

I passed out and in that state, I could hear my dad's voice say, 'You'll be fine. Just rest and you will be up again and getting on with your work.' He used to send us with household goods to our grandmother, who lived in the rural area and when he was constructing a house, sometimes we had to take the construction material on our own, using local buses. You could ask me to do anything but not to go to the rural areas! I loathed it—not because I was just a town girl, but because of the process of getting there.

Firstly, you had to get on what is called a *chicken bus*. These are rural buses that people catch to go to rural places, so the passengers carry many things, including live chickens, eggs … literally anything! Secondly, you not only had to get on one full bus, but you had to stop at this big station and wait for hours before catching the last bus to the rural areas, including to my home area. I could never understand it. You see, some of these buses were filthy, but oddly, they were filled with happy people, who were usually eating something. It was probably a big deal for people to get on a bus and travel to the rural areas. People would laugh and joke—really happy people, and there was no threat at all or feeling out of place. You would find one or two people wanting to help. It would be school holidays and we knew it was rural time. I now know why he always wanted us to go home; to spend time with my grandmother. She missed her grandchildren.

My mum used to say, you need to learn a different life and appreciate the other life, the hard life of living in the rural area. We used to fetch water in the well as compared to free-flowing water from the taps in the city. Bathing was done at the river, where you run the risk of being seen naked by the boys herding cattle! Cooking was done on fire as there was no electricity in our little thatched round kitchen. We were using cow dung to line the walls of my grandmother's kitchen as a cheap thermal insulator. We would spray the fresh cow dung mixed with water to repel insects. Sometimes we would use the dried cow dung as replacement for firewood and also use it to polish the kitchen floor. Talk of creating sustainable homes!

On one particular day, my dad called us together and said one of us had to stay behind in the city, and then go a few days later to take some materials on a bus to our home in the village. We used to drive with him most of the time, but sometimes we would all catch the various buses to travel to the village. My sisters both looked at me with that look that says, 'You thought you were off the hook.' It was my turn. My heart sank. I could see my sisters looking at me with their laughing smiles. My dad indicated it was my turn. You didn't dare say no. I was about eighteen and in high school, not that it made it better. Chicken bus! Plus, going during school holidays was the worst experience. I loved my grandmother but not travelling to see her this way.

I had to get some window frames and door frames on top of the bus, with the help of one of the drivers who was busy fixing the car. As usual, the station was packed with people travelling all over. The bus was taking forever to leave, and I had sat next to a woman with four children, all chewing maize meal and African bubblegum (Xakuxaku in Ndebele language). I greeted her and immediately buried myself in a book, as the music was loud. In those days, there were no earphones. The bus was going far, and I had to stop somewhere in the middle, about 250 kilometres away. You had to be quick lest the bus would leave with your stuff. I had to learn to think quickly. I would have to speak to the conductor, who would get the boys to help offload my items. We arrived around midday at this station in a semi-village, which was crowded with even more people than at the original station.

Then I had to take all the stuff that was on the bus. I waited for my connecting bus but no bus came. I waited and waited and waited. Now I was getting worried. There were no cell phones in those days, nothing at all. I asked a gentleman to look after my goods while I went to look for a lady, a relative who I remembered had a nearby vegetable stall. It was now getting dark and I knew I had to think fast. Luckily, I knew where she lived, because her stall was gone. I went to the house and found her. She helped me with all my stuff and I waited at her house. The bus never arrived as I learned later it that it had broken down. Luckily, my dad's car got fixed earlier than expected, and he passed by this lady's house late at night and found me there, and we drove to the village together. It shows how my dad just believed that I would be okay, and how one must be resilient and think fast, rather than wait for life to happen.

* * *

I woke up with a start. 'Where am I?' My thoughts were racing. I remembered that I had passed out at a clinic a few kilometres from Collahuasi in Chile. I had a headache and was feeling tired. As I lay there, I noted that the nurses were lovely and were, of course, speaking Spanish. We had only one translation booklet, from English to Spanish, and my colleague, Robert, had taken it with him. All I knew was *hola* and *gracias*. I should have taken a course in Spanish. The company did provide classes, and all were paid for. I was thinking about my mum as I lay in bed, and I could hear her say, 'This is not a job for women. I told you. You should have been a nurse.' The *I am not good enough* belief system started creeping in. I was exhausted and all I wanted was to return home and be with my son.

After what felt like ages, but was probably only three hours, the smiling nurse was replaced by another one. As I looked around, I heard a familiar voice calling my name. It was Robert who had come back from the mining processing operation. I pretended to be fast asleep. I just thought he would think I was such a cry baby. But the first thing he said was, 'Are you okay, Patience?' That was such a kind gesture. I heard him stumble through his Spanish. He looked up at me. 'Oh my god! You okay? What happened? How are you feeling?' I mumbled something and he just said, 'It's okay.'

The doctor came and asked him to leave as they needed to check me one more time before I was discharged. I smiled back at the doctor who said something in Spanish, but he could speak English as well. Thank God! The doctor said, 'You are strong woman! Work in mine? Very strong woman. Very good company you work for there, very good.' He kept saying it as if to assure me that I was in good hands. I have always had a small body frame and am short. I never gained much weight those days. I remember when I was younger, I would ask my mum why I was short and if God could make me taller. My mum would tell me that God would not be happy if I asked him to change the way he had created me, and instead, to be happy and to thank God for everything he had given me.

After I was discharged, we drove back to Iquique, and then the following day we still had three more operations to complete. There was the Mantos Blancos mine, which is a large copper mine located in northern Chile in Antofagasta Region, and the Los Bronces mine, another large copper mine. By the time we went back to Santiago, I was already tired and wanted to be back home with my family. We had to undertake dewatering studies and benchmark the efficiencies of the various plants. I remember our last visit was at one of the largest tailings dams in the world. It was like a lake. It was Escondido, another copper mine. Despite the altitude, I enjoyed the culture and all the nice wines. Apart from my time in Australia, this was my first experience outside the country for a mining company. It was a case of a company believing you are capable and competent, and giving you an opportunity.

However, I had no life-work balance. This sentiment is shared by many women I have interviewed. Some prefer to call it integration. Remote workplaces can be very difficult for many women in male-dominated workplaces, which is why most women are reluctant to take on challenging tasks. Reviewing and benchmarking best practice for tailings across all operations was challenging and exciting, but I never prepared myself for leaving my son and being unable to hug him, or help him with homework. I could deal with the challenges of working on heights. We had to carry a bucket and get the water samples and doing these measurements was the easier part. I have the deepest respect for women who work at the *rock face,* as it's called.

This explains why there were not many women working underground in those years back. My few underground experiences were sufficient for me to say, I choose not to work underground. However, now technology is changing the face of the mining industry, creating perfect opportunities to attract more women in STEM. The question is how quickly companies want to adopt the technology that not only will save lives but also will be more efficient and sustainable. My experience at Anglo American made me aware that some of the barriers to women's promotion resides in the inability for them to work in remote places. This then makes male counterparts take on more challenging, high visibility projects, where they can be seen and get an opportunity to be promoted.

There are so many stereotypes that are barriers to women's advancement to moving into positions traditionally held by men. I considered the cost of getting married and having children—how might I do this when I was struggling with one child? On top of that was the necessity of dealing with the cultural expectations of an African husband and family. Back then, one was penalised for being pregnant, where you are paid less during maternity leave. Such a consequence was not practical for me. It is true that it often takes a village to build a career. I learned to ask for help when I had to raise my son. Sometimes other parents from my son's school were important. Asking for help isn't a sign of weakness. It is a sign of strength. Leaders need to grasp this. True equality and gender diversity will only be achieved when we all fight the invisible barriers that hold women back.

This is why most women in mining prefer to work in less remote places and mostly for one company, as they will have built relationships and have become accustomed to the way things are done. The downside for those who are ambitious and want to rise in the mining industry is that being risk-averse and not getting operational experience can result in stagnation. Bigger organisations, such as Anglo American, provide better opportunities to expand, as one can move across different functional areas internally in the same organisation, instead of switching to a different company. This was the case for me as I switched various roles within the same company, and the different experiences were useful preparation for my leadership journey. Change can be very difficult and, for me, moving to another city or to an operational role would have been personally very difficult.

I finally arrived back home in Johannesburg, tired and exhausted from the long 15-hour flight from Santiago. I wanted to just relax, watch TV, and spend time with my family. It was Friday night when we landed, which was perfect as I needed the weekend break. As I was unwinding in front of the TV, with my son William, sister Diana and brother Tinashe, I reflected on my career journey and what this new role would mean for me. I needed to look after and spend time with my son, especially given I was his only parent. As much as I had Diana and Tinashe during university holidays, I still needed to be there for him. We had our usual pizza day and fun playing tennis, and then as I was gardening, I reflected again on my career. I realised this job with its travelling was going to be very difficult for me.

The transport provided by the school was reliable, but sometimes my sister would be late from university, making it difficult to leave William alone at home when the helper had knocked off. The only possible option I could think of was to send him to a boarding school. The good boarding schools were very expensive but I had saved a lot of my money and was living modestly. My mum always used to say, 'Don't waste money'. I had saved all my money and bought my little townhouse. I didn't have any debts except for the house mortgage. After reflecting deeply and consulting with my mother and sisters, I decided perhaps it was time to start exploring and finding out more about boarding schools. On the other hand, I thought I should still try to get into the strategy department.

Many studies have shown that women only apply for jobs if they think they meet one hundred percent of the criteria listed, while men believe they qualify, even when they meet only around sixty per cent of the requirements. I personally have never thought I'm not ready to do something. My belief is learning by doing. On the following Monday morning as I was going through the mail, I saw an advertisement for a planning analyst, and they wanted someone with an MBA and some process division knowledge. I didn't tick all the boxes, but that was the role I wanted. I applied even though I knew I didn't tick all the boxes as they needed someone with some process division experience. I told myself I would learn on the job. Little did I know that the process division for Platinum is not an easy process and I knew very little except for the concentrators.

I applied, and got an interview. It was a tough interview I must say, as there were three panel members: the divisional director, Peter, the head of strategy, Gordon and the general manager for process who was July that time. I had read, asked other people, and prepared well. I knew my story. They were impressed. They explained that the role would involve having to develop a new process model that would give the process division assumptions to be used for modelling. The existing model was not sufficiently robust and was becoming unstable and very complex. I said I would do it, including investment valuations for the company, and that having completed my MDP, I had a fair understanding of project valuation. I knew I had nailed it.

Two weeks later I was advised I had secured the job. I had already informed my boss and he wasn't happy at all, as we were supposed to be doing the Phase-2 benchmarking work. This time around, we were to travel to the operations around South Africa, Namibia and Zimbabwe. However, I was excited about my new role. My transfer was quickly organised and a month later, I was at 55 Marshall Street at the main head office of Anglo Platinum. I was on the seventh floor, with a beautiful office next to that of Dr Bolha, a very great friend of mine.

Finally, the role I had been visualising myself doing, to integrate my need to take care of my son while working, had manifested. The power of imagination and being crystal clear about where I wanted to be had finally paid off. It goes without saying that just imagining and visualising, without taking massive action, wouldn't have got me there. Most people know that they don't like their work, but when you ask them what they want to do, they don't know the answer. All they know is that they don't like what they are doing. I often coach my clients and ask incisive questions to dig deeper to understand what drives them, what gives them energy and what their highest needs are.

The first month into the role, I quickly adjusted, and I had a few friends that I had met at Anglo Research, and some from the operations section, including Tony Anyimadu, Eunice Matsau and Fortune Mashimbye. I was happy and knew I was at the right place. But no honeymoon lasts forever, which I soon learned the hard way. When I accepted the role, little did I know that I would confront the same difficulty I had for leaving the previous role: I would face the same challenges of having to spend time in the operations in the first few months, but also even during the planning process. There is no way one can work for a mining company without going to the operations, especially in process planning. The good news was that it was not the major part of the role. I would be required to go to the operations for budget reviews, multidisciplinary audits, long-term planning sessions, and so on.

By then, my son was attending St Andrews College, a boarding school in the Eastern Cape in South Africa. My uncle's children all went there, and Tinashe my brother and Tarisai my cousin, were at Rhodes University. William would have the support of his auntie and uncle and St Andrews was one of the best schools in South Africa. Nestled in the small town of Grahamstown, it was a traditional old Anglican private school, within a lovely setting. It was very expensive, and the only way I could fund it was to use my savings at that time. It was a tough call but I paid the fees and the deal was done.

During my three years at the research centre, I learned a lot about client relationships and knowing what the customer wants, which consisted of helping my boss with supporting operations to be more efficient. This skill came in handy when I had to start this new role. My main responsibility was to help develop a new model that would be more robust but, in a way, a predictive model. As I started learning about the current model that was on Excel, I could see it was far more complicated than I thought. I soon knew that the only way to succeed was to go back to the process operations and learn as much as possible. Without the operational experience, it was going to be a very difficult task. I spent time visiting and learning more about the process operations, starting from smelting operations, then spending time in the base metal's refinery, then the magnetic separation plant, and finally the slag-cleaning furnace and the precious metals refinery. I had to understand the entire process division and undertake process mapping in order to develop a robust model. It was not an easy job as I thought initially.

After I had completed the site visits and the process mapping, one of my colleagues resigned from his position in long-term planning. This meant that I was then going to have to focus on long-term planning. Initially, I was focussing on the short-term planning model whose outputs were critical for the business's long-term global assumption period that integrated all functions, including finance.

Working under Dr Gordon Smith and the Strategy and Planning team was again another best experience in my career I have ever had. I was initially the only female, but later was joined by Lana and Bon Mathibe. We were like a girls' club, supported by the experienced senior analysts. It was here that I had the greatest career and personal growth. Being in that department was initially intimidating, as Gordon ensured he recruited the best of the best talent, but I liked his inclusive leadership style. Everyone had a seat at the table with an opportunity to speak at every Monday morning meeting. Bon and I admired the more senior Lana who was poised and well spoken. I was particularly struck by her unshakeable confidence. Bon and I started emulating Lana and slowly but surely, we became more confident. If you want to succeed in life, role model someone you admire.

I was still the process planning analyst working with the planning division, with the executive head and his general managers, and then with all the planning guys, to develop the investment proposals. What the job really entailed was doing the short-term budget and also focussing on creating the group global assumptions, and then developing all the project valuations for that division. It was a great experience. Not only did I build important relationships during that period, but all those networks that I had built over the years in the operations became handy, as I still had to work with them, and particularly when it came to multidisciplinary audits and investment project valuation.

The project team were the clients because they were the owners of the projects, and we were working collaboratively, doing the investment valuation of the capital projects. Because the role involved a lot of strategy, finance, economics and accounting, I decided it was time to complete an MBA, as I think I was one of the few without one in the department. Because I had completed an MDP, with three distinctions, I was exempted from my first year, then joining the class in second year. I always strive to be the best in everything I do. I was surprised when I received the Dean's List Award for both my second and third years, and I became a member of the Golden Key International Honours Society for having the highest academic scores. I also won the Standard Bank Entrepreneurship Award.

We were 15 MBA students who had to present to some six or so Venture Capitalists (VC). I prepared my business plan and presentation. At that time, Anglo American was rolling out Xstrata's Isa Mills across their operations. I knew the grinding media was sourced overseas and then a thought came to me: *What if we get the grinding media manufactured locally, and we partner with the current company producing it?* I felt I had nailed it. I was quite confident that I had won but was very nervous. When we had all presented our business plans, we waited for the outcome; my heart was pounding. The business case made sense as the venture capitalists were going to invest, and the balance I had put in partnership with IDC would fund the project. The financials and assumptions, including sensitivities, were very modest. The case was clear.

The MC stood up and started talking about how all business plans were very good and made the VC job very difficult. I wasn't listening. I just wanted to get it over with and, before I knew it, I heard, 'The winner for this round of the Entrepreneur Award is …(silence)… Dr Patience Mpofu.' I was excited, shocked and happy. I stood to collect the certificate and the cheque from Standard Bank. This award was based on the top student who presented the best, fundable and profitable business plan to the panel of investors. I subsequently founded a company, Insight Africa Investments and Consulting, to start the business. This was a huge achievement. We spoke about the next step, and the VC indicated that I needed to secure a letter from the company that they would consider switching suppliers. There were several steps as part of the implementation plan that I put forward, and the first was to engage the company with the proposal. As I speak now, there are many local manufacturers who later executed such a business.

As I was putting together a proposal and trying to set up a meeting with various people, the 2007–2008 global financial crisis (GFC) hit. Everything came to a standstill; it was business *un*usual with the total collapse of all companies. It was survival time. I was devastated, as not only was my entrepreneurial journey cut short, but I was at risk of losing my job too. What was I to do about my son's education? I had just signed up for a development to build my new house. My existing place was becoming smaller, especially when my mum or sisters were visiting. In my African culture, you accommodate everyone. I needed a place with a bigger garden, a bigger pool and an extra bedroom for my mum and visitors. I was staying with my brother and my son at that time. Due to the 2009 global economic crisis, the business could not get investment from the funders.

The GFC was one of the most severe worldwide financial crises. The excessive lending by banks, resulted in a housing bubble in the USA thus impacting financial institutions globally. This triggered a Great Recession, followed by the European debt crisis. The GFC was a turning point for me, as the global financial crisis had a severe impact on South Africa. The South African economy went into recession in 2008/09 for the first time in 17 years.The mining industry was no exception. Cynthia Carroll had been in the role as CEO for Anglo American for less than a year when the GFC hit. She was one of only three female chief executives of FTSE 100 companies. Three years in a row, from 2007–2009, she was ranked by *Forbes* magazine as the fifth most powerful woman in the world. She stepped down in October 2012.

Having a role model in life can easily shift your perspective. You will see how the appointment of a female CEO in the industry shifted mine.

Exercise

Having a career strategy is critical, as is building a network of relationships. What are you known for in your job? I recall, I developed an innovative robust model for valuing capital projects in the process division. Suddenly, I became the go to person in that area. It all boils down to making an impact and consistently delivering beyond expectation.

Go to www.unleashingmysuperpowers.com/bonuses for a free download of a template on how to create career strategy.

CHAPTER 5

WHY WE NEED
MORE FEMALE ROLE MODELS

It's not the strongest that will survive, nor the most intelligent.
It's the most adaptable to change.
– Charles Darwin

Because of You, by B.G. Hennessy

Each time a child is born, the world changes.
When you were born, there was a new person for your family to love and care for.
And because of you, there is one more person who can love and care for others.
Because of you, there is one more person who will grow and learn and one more person who can teach others.
Because of you, there is one more person to share with.
And there is one more person who can share feelings and ideas, as well as things.
Because of you, there is one more person who needs help and one more person who can help the others.
When you help, care, share, and listen, you are being kind.
When two people help, care, share and listen to each other, they are friends.

When people from different countries help, care, share, and listen to one another, it is called peace.
Even something as big and important as peace begins with something small and precious. It might begin… because of you.
When she finally unleashes her superpowers, it is… because of you.

My entire career has only been in the mining industry, where I have had the privilege of working in various roles at some of the top ten mining companies globally. Throughout that journey, I have learned so much about leadership: a hot topic while the COVID-19 pandemic ravages our lives. Many of us believe we're not getting the leaders we need, as we see questionable leadership in many aspects of our lives during the pandemic. What expectations do we have of our leaders?

As someone who has spent a lot of time in Africa and who loves wild life photography, this makes me ponder what leaders might learn from the animal kingdom. I've absorbed quite a lot from those amazing safari trips during my holidays and the ensuing debates about leadership in the animal kingdom. There is so much to learn there, with new and fascinating perspectives on leadership. Animals, like humans, thrive or fail depending on the quality of their leadership.

What makes a good leader in the animal kingdom? What are the most common traits of great animal leaders? Why do animals follow a particular leader? My favourite animal is the lion. Its majestic presence exudes and epitomises a leader who is quiet and yet powerful. Most importantly, its leadership characteristic shows a certain remarkable trait that we can learn from.

I learned so much at the Ulusaba Safari Lodge, one of the best safari lodges I have ever been to. It is Sir Richard Branson's private game reserve in South Africa. The name Ulusaba means *place of little fear*, so named because the kopje, or hill, on which Rock Lodge sits provided the ancient Shangaan tribal warriors with the perfect lookout point. Ulusaba has the most beautiful lodges, which sit entirely within the Sabi Sand Reserve near Kruger National Park. People visit the area for the abundant game and the variety of sightings possible. Once experienced, you will be hooked. We visited Ulusaba not once but three times, and have been to their three lodges. Your chances of seeing the big five animals are highly likely in this safari lodge, although it depends mostly on the time of year you visit.

One of the things I did was give myself and my family incentives to work harder if we achieved our goals. This trip was one of those. South Africa is one of the most beautiful places to visit. Not only are the people friendly, but the climate is glorious most of the time. From breathtaking scenery on the garden route, the bustling vibrant city culture in Johannesburg, wild safaris in the Kruger National Park in Mpumalanga Province, to sun-soaked coastal beaches in Durban or the Atlantic Seaboard in Western Cape, it represents the best travel value for money. My favourite regions are Mpumalanga and KwaZulu Natal, because of the breathtaking views and wildlife safaris. No other place in the world has these types of heritage sites.

We would leave early in the morning, taking about six hours to reach our destination, as we would have several stops on the way for sightseeing. I was struck by the excellent service at Ulusaba, from the minute we first arrived at reception, where you sip champagne while you wait for a short time before riding on the safari bus to your lodge.

On one such occasion, the guide told us there was a pride of lions that had just killed a buffalo, and we should get ready so as not to miss the game drive. We needed no encouragement and in a short space of time, we were ready. As usual, the guide and spotter were friendly, and we went straight to the site and saw the pride of lions: two females, eight cubs and one male. Each day that we passed the area, we could see how new animals came in for the meat, from vultures to hyenas.

We can learn a lot about leadership from lions, by studying their behaviour and within their prides. The first thing that strikes me all the time when I see a lion especially a male one, is its presence and magnificent appearance which can be intimidating. Its strength is evident: so fierce and bold. I love watching the lion! It's a special animal, and I understand why it is referred to as the king of the jungle. Lions have fascinating character traits that include courage, strength and decisiveness, which are also the main traits that can make you stand out as a great leader. They are also social animals as they live in large groups called prides. These groups normally consist of lionesses—whose role is to hunt—their cubs, and lions who are there to protect the pride.

We need bold leadership. As a leader, you need to be visible, and stand out like a lion. If you develop a reputation for being caring with your teams, for example, your boldness will increase as well. How often do leaders protect their teams? As a leader, teams need to feel valued and cared for. That's true leadership as epitomised by the lion and lioness.

Male lion at Ulusaba Safari Lodge

As we visited the site over the next few days, we found the lions sleeping most of the time. Lions can sleep for over 20 hours. How often do we leaders sacrifice our sleep, working through the night with no rest? Finding time to rest your mind, body and soul is super important. Taking time to reflect as a leader is important. Towards the end of our trip, the lions were not touching the carcass of the kill. On day 2, we witnessed vultures feeding on the remains, then on our last day, it was hyenas. Lions rarely eat the entire prey, usually leaving leftovers for other animals like hyenas and vultures. Are you a leader who shares with others? When a lion roars, everyone pays attention. Boldness does not mean you are always aggressive. But it means that everything you do or say should be remarkable and powerful to capture everyone's attention. Be bold for a change. Be bold about your passion!

It is interesting to observe that wild animals will follow a leader they can trust to keep them safe. As humans, we have the same expectations of our leaders.

The other impressive animal I love is the elephant, which is my totem. The matriarch is usually the oldest and largest female elephant and the leader of the herd. I love elephants for their caring nature and empathy. They are well known for working effectively as a team as they also move as a herd. They can sense when another elephant needs help, and they are good at cooperating with each other. Elephants are excellent examples of animals that demonstrate great leadership qualities such as cooperation, teamwork, collaboration, determination and empathy. Clearly, there are great leadership qualities to be learned from lions and elephants. What strikes me as significant is the slightly different styles of leadership, especially between a male lion and female elephant. To me, the female elephant epitomises the leadership style of women, which is the kind we need right now to lead in the twenty-first century. This has been witnessed during the COVID-19 pandemic.

How Do Women Lead That Makes Their Leadership Style Unique and Relevant for the 21st Century?

This extract is taken from an article written by Wittenberg-Cox (2020). She chose examples of some commonalities of powerful women across the globe who led their countries during the pandemic. There are some lessons that male leaders of mining companies could reflect on and learn from, regarding how these women succeeded in their leadership paths. The main components identified were trust, decisiveness and love. 'What I found very interesting is these women were much more ready and comfortable expressing love and care while leading,' says Wittenberg-Cox. The major learnings and important actions of these women leaders are summarised below. Leaders can use and adapt these objectives to create an environment that is inclusive, especially in uncertain times.

- Be inclusive. The most successful leaders include everyone in their plans.
- Be an authentic leader. The pandemic made many of us more aware of the struggles of others, especially in developing countries where inequality is still rampant.
- Be truthful, as truth builds trust.
- Use technology to connect with your teams. The pandemic showed us that technology offers diverse communications solutions.

In summary, great leaders inspire, revealing and empowering others to become great leaders.

Power and strength behaviours demonstrated by the patriarchy and masculinity are not required traits for leadership in the 21st century, as demonstrated by women leaders during COVID-19. Technology makes it easier for almost anyone to work anywhere. The old days of hard labour in mining, such as that of the drill operator, are numbered. What technology will do is change the way we work, thus creating more opportunities for women to work in previously male-dominated work environments. We have seen this with the COVID-19 pandemic and how it has created a new norm with remote working and acceleration of digital technology. An epiphany moment in my leadership journey was how I experienced being led for the first time by a female, in one of the largest mining companies in the world.

The Power of Relationships and Visibility

Moving into the strategy department at Anglo Platinum was a game changer for me. This career change involved expanding my business and management knowledge to broaden my experience, from solving complex business problems to client relationship development. As we were all dealing with this GFC shock event, the company had to do some restructuring to protect the balance sheet. A temporary role became available in the program office in Johannesburg. I just knew that something was going on, and I decided to speak with the head of that office, Archie Myezwa. He offered me the role.

Anglo valued intellectual integrity and this role stretched my abilities. I found the work satisfying and I enjoyed the challenge of engaging with really super smart people, and producing high quality work that had an impact. The opportunity to participate in strategic issues for the organisation, and working as part of the global team, was priceless. I became a resourceful person and quickly built my leadership capabilities. My demonstrated industrial experience in managing and implementing research projects came in handy when working on strategic options for the organisation. Role models for other women are important. I had a role model: the CEO, who happened to be a female.

When Cynthia Carroll became the new CEO for Anglo American, Anglo Platinum's safety record had gone through the roof prior to that. Her leadership presence on safety was notable. Within a few weeks, she stopped the Rustenburg operations for safety reasons. No such shutdown had ever been undertaken before in the mining industry and it was not a popular decision. The Platinum CEO left the company a few weeks later. Cynthia had brought in a fresh perspective and a different kind of leadership.

True leaders live on in the hearts and minds of their teams. I still remember vividly how Cynthia changed the entire safety culture of the organisation, as explained above. Talk about leaders walking the talk. We went through thorough training on safety procedures, with campaigning and communication of the new way towards zero harm throughout the entire company to rolling out new safety procedures. For the first time, I started being aware of how some of my own unconscious behaviours were contributing to unsafe hazards. For example, some of the visible things we started seeing were as simple as walking along the stairs with three-point contact. Anyone found violating safety rules would be in trouble. We spent most of our time at head office, but the presence was hugely felt in the new safety culture. She transformed the culture of safety while I was working there.

Great leadership requires courage and boldness, and Cynthia was courageous and epitomised the leadership qualities we should all admire and model. She is a truly visionary, inspirational leader, which are characteristics that, for me, makes a huge difference in whether I think one is a great leader or not. There were few that inspired me to do more. If your actions inspire others to dream more, learn more, do more and become more, you are a great leader. That year was the company's best for safety, according to Anglo American Platinum's annual report. The number of fatalities was halved from 25 miners in 2007, to 12 in 2011, and then halved again in 2013. The goal is always zero harm. She indeed is a leader who is a force for good, and she is now on the Board of Glencore as a non-executive director.

What Does a Peak Performance Leader for the 21st Century Look Like?

What makes an effective and successful leader? In my view, an effective and successful leader leads themselves in self-mastery, challenges their own belief systems that might limit them from leading effectively and inspiring others, and finally has the mental and spiritual toughness to build great teams and create peak performance organisations. A successful leader makes everyone (including stakeholders) feel heard and respected, is inclusive, and values the diversity of each and every member of their team or organisation. Ultimately, they have the power and ability to identify and unleash each person's superpowers to be the better versions of themselves so that they create even more value for all stakeholders. Critical Executive management skills are super important. This is the ability to influence and persuade peers and subordinates to support your point of view.

Visionary thinking and the ability to conceptualise the future of the organisation, is a complex skill requiring a broad perspective, the ability to integrate multiple points of view, and a talent to look into the future, or to think strategically (Fels 2004). Is brave enough to dream big and smart enough to climb step by step. Cognitive mastery is important, as is intellectual mastery and emotional mastery. Male patriarchy and masculinity to prove power and strength is not required as a trait for leadership in the 21st century.

A leader who is people-centric and has foresight, and to a certain degree, possesses what I call infinite intelligence. An enlightened leader has empathy, humility and spiritual intelligence and is compassionate with themself and others. A leader brings unity, and has a high level of consciousness. It's about humanity. At the end of the day, each leader needs to think about ensuring they don't destroy people, as this fosters disharmony. My inspiration are leaders with a high level of consciousness, like Nelson Mandela and Oprah Winfrey.

How important is effective leadership in achieving actual change and productivity in an organisation? Leadership is at the core of any organisation and it is the leader who defines its culture. If the culture promotes non-delivery, poor engagement, value destruction, and an uncaring attitude towards its stakeholders and so forth, all these will filter across the entire organisation. We need leaders who are visionary, compassionate and empathetic, with high levels of consciousness; leaders who value their employees and communities, and create sustainable shared value. Employees can only function productively if they are supported in their wellness. We have seen how COVID-19 has impacted everyone, including their mental health.

What questions are leaders not asking themselves? We need to start asking the right questions and challenge ourselves about our assumptions about the world. Anyone wanting to advance in their career, nurture their talents, and take on more leadership roles should know their *why* and their values, and believe in themselves as a leader. Constantly seek feedback on your behaviours to improve your leadership skills and relationship building. Investing in a coach and a mentor who will help you navigate your challenges and support you. Leadership is a journey, and constantly learning is vital, as we live in uncertain times. This is an inspiration that each person reading this can draw strength from.

My mother is truly my leadership hero. She is someone who has humility. True leaders always aim to serve rather than be served. Being humble makes you more approachable to your followers and allows you to create an environment of open communication and more effective feedback. She has empathy, which plays a critical role in one's ability to be a successful leader. It sharpens your *people acumen* and allows leaders to develop and maintain relationships with those they lead. They possess high emotional intelligence (EQ). Leaders who possess this trait always make time for people.

Great leaders are able to define their vision and inspire it in others, to ensure the sustainable growth of an organisation. They communicate their vision in such a way that it motivates their teams. There is clarity of how success look. They are great communicators: quick to listen and slow to speak. One should never hear of upcoming changes via the grapevine. I remember one occasion and one leader in particular, where a huge announcement was made that was only impacting roles in his department. He had a meeting that morning and said, 'I had no idea about this huge change.' I just wondered how a major change, which impacts one of your team members, can be made without your knowledge. Something was amiss. There are sometimes good bosses in a bad company, but I would prefer to work for a great leader in any company, good or bad. A good leader will stand up for you, trust you, listen to you and even make a bad job enjoyable. There is nothing compared to knowing your manager has your back.

There were seven of us in the strategy team at Anglo Platinum, and we had a reporting line to the group head of strategy, Heike Truol. This was collaboration and global teamwork at its best. Bear in mind, it was just after the GFC, and balance sheets and cash preservation were the order of the day. Cynthia introduced a new way of doing strategy. Every decision had to be rigorously analysed to ensure there was no value leakage. We would produce the industry and competitor analysis that was well received across the organisation for the platinum sector. My colleagues and I had a great working relationship, including with our boss. We all had various accountabilities to support our functional executive heads. Working with best-in-class people in problem solving made us feel challenged and recognised, and it was global but still local. Working in strategy provides you with key strategic skills. How much time you spend on your own, working and building relationships or networking, becomes more relevant. Strategy gave us the aerial view while still balancing the detailed work of financial models. It is important to strike a balance.

Understanding the business model and the competitive environment was critically important. Mining is a capital-intensive industry, and one of the major projects I had to work on with consultants was on project prioritisation. This was critical, as the capital spend had to be slashed due to subdued commodity prices. This role was very senior as one had to learn to manage and build relationships. Advocacy and influencing became the order of the day as visibility mattered. I learned the importance to build a network and alliances beyond your usual people because now you touch every part of the organisation, and without the relationships, you are doomed.

Working with some of the top talented people not only helps you think smarter but it unleashes your superpowers. Working with super smart people who challenge you is refreshing. I thrive in those environments where I am intellectually stimulated. We had to mentor the strategy analysts working with us, so collaboration and teamwork was critical. We were constantly learning but also learning to say, 'I don't know'. Working with executives on projects and in processing was a great learning curve. I had to deliver and ensure I provided value and impact for their functions. Off-sites strategies were critical for the department as a deliverable.

This was where the social capital became even more relevant, inherent in the power of relationships and networking. We were directly working with Exco and the global strategy team in London, which gave us a bigger overview. Problem-solving skills were tested here as one would get key strategic questions straight from the CEO to answer. Our leader used to say, *Never destroy my relationships*. That was his mantra. We developed great friendships and relationships with our stake-holders. But the most impactful phenomenon was working with the most amazing women leaders. I met amazing women, including my colleague, Bon Mathibe who to this day remains a great friend. We were certainly inspired by leaders including Deshnee Naidoo and Heike Truol, who worked closely with Cynthia Carroll. Cynthia set a leadership benchmark and has inspired more.

This was one of the best experiences, which took me to the next level of growth. Those were the special moments I still hold dear from this company in which I spent more than ten years. It doesn't take much to create those special moments with your team. Good bosses are few and far between, but if and when you get one, you should really appreciate them. This is why we need more female role model leaders to inspire and unleash the superpowers of other women in male-dominated work environments, including in mining. She indeed unleashed my superpowers!

Exercise

Clarity of goals is critical in achieving success as a leader: Answer the following and write your answers down:

1. What are your top 1–3 goals (outcomes) you would like to achieve in the next three months?
2. These must be SMART: Specific, Measurable, Achievable, Realistic and Time Bound.
3. What can get in the way?
4. How will you know you have achieved your goal? What does success look like?

Download a free copy of a goal setting template from
www.unleashingmysuperpowers.com/bonuses

CHAPTER 6

THE GLASS CUSHION

*I realised if I wait to be called in the room to sit at the table and lean
in, I will wait forever. I unleashed my superpowers.*
– Dr Patience Mpofu

The Glass Cushion, by Dr Patience Mpofu

They said work hard,
Very hard and success is guaranteed
I worked hard with GRIT
I succeeded

I kept walking up the stairs, then fell on the way.
I asked the universe, God, why
But who is in your corner? she asked
Hmmm, Ahmm I mumbled
Only my boss, I answered
You got your answer
You need more supporters, a network, a tribe, female preferably, to lift
you up

I did what I was told, got more supporters
I succeeded and rose up again
Shortly afterwards, I fell again
Went back again, I am powerless, I don't know what to do
How do you spend your time? she asked
I said I spend it working hard to deliver
Then you got your answer, go and advocate and lean in
I asked, what is that?
Speak about your achievements to those who matter, she said

I did what I was told, succeeded, then fell again shortly afterwards
I asked the universe, God, what do I do next, I am stuck
Do you have a coach, she asked. No?
Do you have a mentor, she asked?
I said no
Go get a coach and a mentor
I got both and I got promoted and started walking up the stairs
But there was something as I was about to reach the top
It was a glass ceiling, I got stuck and could not go further

God then opened a door and revealed to me something
Something I never knew existed
A glass cushion, inside this glass cushion,
Was a man, looking relaxed
Around him were many other males cheering him up
He was relaxed, happy and feeling supported
While I have been working hard all along
I was stunned

Barriers to Women's Advancement in the Mining Industry: Survey Results

Some studies have shown that the advice to women to *lean in* and be more confident doesn't help, whereas that research showed that confidence matters for men's job promotion prospects. But for women, *leaning in* provides no guarantee of a payoff, according to Risse (2020). She says, being more confident and more ambitious, like a man, can actually make you the enemy of not only men but also some females.

Facebook executive Sandberg (2013), through her book, *Lean In*, shows that women are hindered by barriers that exist within themselves, through lacking self-confidence, by not raising their hands, and by pulling back when they should be leaning in. In my view as a woman in STEM from the mining industry and from a culturally different environment, showing confidence may work against you sometimes. Confidence matters to a certain extent but is frowned upon when one is a black woman. Displaying confidence in myself has worked sometimes but not other times. However, having said that, I believe there are more benefits than not showing your confidence. I believe the confidence one needs to have is about knowing oneself, and when to walk away. Showing too much confidence and speaking up has to be done strategically. It's an internal unshakeable inner strength that ties with self-belief, emotional intelligence, rather than more of just an outward trait.

There are many invisible barriers that hold females back from succeeding to C-Suite when working in male-dominated workplaces, particularly as they move up the ladder. We did a survey of 100 women, which revealed some of the challenges women are facing, particularly in the mining industry as the sample had more than 65% women from this industry. A huge barrier and challenge for women below the C-Suite position is that after working twice as hard, when it is time for a promotion, they are overlooked. They constantly have to prove themselves, despite their experience. This is further worsened when a male counterpart with less experience is promoted. The question is does a glass cushion actually exist in male-dominated workplaces such as the mining industry?

I can relate to this pain as I went through such an experience, despite having delivered one of the most important KPIs of the organisation I was working for. I was hoping to be promoted but was disappointed when I was told I was not ready. When will women ever be ready? This sort of situation is where you start seeing the glass cushion and the boys' club emerging.

My three-year plan with Anglo Platinum turned into more than ten years, with three years in an operational role and more than six years in strategy and planning. I learned more than I could ever have dreamed in my life; working with great strategists and leaders. I eventually felt that I had stayed long enough and it was time to move on to something new and more challenging. Negotiation skill was what I was looking for. Then an opportunity for a much more senior and bigger role became available for me at one of the third largest platinum producers. I contemplated the offer deeply, as it meant leaving an organisation in which I had grown and built a career for close to twelve years.

It was a difficult decision, but on the other hand, it provided a broader and more exciting part of my career, in which I badly wanted to learn and grow: the M&A space for the mining industry. In strategy, we would explore potential opportunities for value creation and present these opportunities, but we had to hand it over to business development to further execute. My career was initially not a straight line. I remained almost at the same level until I later got promoted. But I was navigating the corporate environment, accumulating various skills that ended up getting me to where I wanted to be.

There is no *one* way to get to C-Suite, there are various ways to get there. In particular, with the new skills of the future and digital technology, one can navigate various roles at the same levels, and achieve satisfaction, while keeping eyes on career goals. One common way has been to do an MBA, then switch careers, especially in male-dominated workplaces. That is exactly what I did. My career was not a straight line, but it allowed me to meet very interesting people and gave me a sense of progress and fulfillment. I knew I needed to get a more senior role elsewhere, to experience different cultures and to meet new people in order to expand my network.

As mentioned before, I had a career strategy, and I realised that a gap in my skills and experience was in the area of commercial transaction or closing a deal. Besides, I was passionate about the M&A space. I had met the chief commercial officer and knew him a bit from the mining social circles. I went through the interview process and was offered the job of Senior Manager Business Development and Strategy. I was excited, as it would offer great prospects and new learnings in business development and transactions, but most importantly, I would be learning how to close deals, especially the Black Economic Empowerment (BEE) deals, which was the KPI. I have always been deliberate about my career goals. I somehow knew that I needed change.

The longer I stayed, doing more or less the same things, the more it would hamper my career ambitions. However, sometimes careers do not need to be mapped out in such a way that they become rigid, as you may miss out on great opportunities. You need to be agile, especially now with the world changing daily and becoming more unpredictable. My career was not exactly where I visualised it to be in the initial stages. It has evolved with the changing times, which is also what is more important to me. Treating your career goals just like a company business plan is super important. I have always been driven by solving organisational problems and making an overall greater impact. The bigger the problem, the more I felt fulfilled. Strategy was my passion as it gave me the opportunity to think outside the box and solve a problem. Business development was going to then add to the execution of the strategy, which is what I lacked.

I was fortunate again to report to a really nice manager. As I reflect in hindsight, I have never had a leader with whom I didn't get along so well, except maybe one. He was pleasant and we built a good rapport. I met all the team members, including the CEO and the entire Exco, as I was going to coordinate the strategy off-site session. I seemed to fit in well and I was generally happy.

I was reporting to the Vice President of Business Development, responsible for identifying, evaluating and developing value accretive asset options and opportunities globally, and for the identification and analysis of commercial opportunities for mergers and acquisitions internationally. It involved leading internal and external teams assisting in the transaction, like the legal and financial advisors, to help us structure the transactions, evaluate options, and develop commercial negotiating strategies and positions. They would also assist with the due diligence processes and final implementation of the transactions.

I was also accountable for coordinating the strategic planning process, working closely with the strategy committee and executive committee (Exco), on the development of the corporate strategies, ensuring the process was stimulating, challenging and balanced between near-term opportunities and blue-sky thinking. Influencing and managing the important stakeholders was a big part of the transaction, which included other mining industries, government institutions, the regulators, and such. I had to prepare Exco and board papers for approval, and presentations for the CEO, and sometimes also externally, as part of lobbying. It was an exciting and challenging role. What made it even more challenging was that the company had to complete three transactions that are part of what is called the Broad-Based Socio-Economic Empowerment Charter for the Mining Industry, known as the Mining Charter.

I have worked predominantly in South Africa, therefore, some of my references will be from well published sources on policy there. The Minerals Council South Africa, through its website, reports that the mining industry has had a significantly positive impact on the economy in South Africa. To redress the imbalances, which are the consequences of some legacies of apartheid, the Mining Charter framework was pioneered and implemented in 2004 by the DMRE.

The main objective has been to facilitate meaningful participation of HDSAs in the mining and minerals industry, by deracialising ownership of the industry, expanding business opportunities for HDSAs, and enhancing the social and economic welfare of employees and mine communities (Minerals Councils, South Africa website). This has helped to get more women to participate in the industry at various levels. This is at the core of the social licence to operate, to comply with the charter, making it one of the few countries to have a policy to redress gender inequality in the sector.

Thus, the company I was working for was involved in increasing equity ownership to HDSA, from 18 % equity to 26 %. That was our role in business development, amongst other commercial transactions, and in coordinating the strategy session for the company. It was a lot of work and was required to be delivered within a short period of time. My first 90 days passed so quickly, as I was busy preparing for the strategy off-site session. This was my accountability and I was co-ordinating various work streams across the organisation with the Exco and their heads of department. It was not an easy task, considering I was still new, and bringing a new way of doing strategy. Meanwhile, my boss was working on engaging advisors for the three critical transactions that we had to work on. That strategy session never happened on the intended day. In addition, it was with a different focus and mood. A strike had started at our mining operations. Little did we know, this was not only going to change the employees but the entire country, to being in the spotlight forever.

The day that changed our lives, in August 2012, is a day that made me, and others, question our existence. It was the day of the Marikana incident, where 34 miners were killed during a strike. We started asking ourselves very difficult questions. It was not at all what we had expected. I was affected and didn't know what to do, and the incident led me to learn a lot about crisis management. Marikana was a crisis that changed the company forever and was a turning point in my career. I had just been in the new company and role for three months. Did I make the right decision? You see, decisions determine our destiny. It is in those moments of a crisis that sometimes our purpose is revealed. It dawned on me that the mining industry was facing complex challenges and problems involving various stakeholders.

In the 6 months that followed, it was a crisis and most of the work was on crises management. The company had to restructure as the share price plummeted. When people talk about the value of reputation of an organisation, this is where you realise that organisations have to continuously review, reflect particularly the values and culture they have and how it is perceived. The company does not exist anymore. It was finally acquired by another global mining company with a stronger balance sheet. The question is what are some of the lessons to be learnt? Leaders need to unlearn, relearn and continuously improve on their performance when it comes to sustainability.

The Biggest Growth Comes From the Biggest Pain

When Marikana happened, stagnation crept in. On a personal level, I had an emergency medical operation and went on medical leave, and as much as it was not easy to recover while not knowing what lay ahead, I had time to reflect. With some introspection after the emotional trauma and empathy at the time, I started asking myself some challenging questions about transformational leadership, sustainability, the shared value concept, and such deep philosophical enquiries. Questions that crossed my mind were: What am I here for in regard to my values and beliefs? How can I become a true catalyst for a better world? How could we create a shared value for all stakeholders? What would I want to be remembered for when I leave this earth? I set more personal goals for learning new skills in the next three years.

In my personal life, I am someone who embraces uncertainty. In my professional life, I learned to accept uncertainty and even to embrace it. Dealing with uncertainty is a skill. Many people prefer to stay with what they know. COVID-19 has shown us how important it is to be agile. Following the incident, the organisation had to restructure. We all had to reapply for our jobs, and I recall my job had many applicants, as some roles became redundant. I didn't know if I would have a role after this.

As I lay in bed planning, I received an email regarding an opportunity to serve at my former business school. The Wits Business School (WBS) launched and offered the Post-Master's Certificate Program in Leadership to MBA alumni as a means of developing coaching skills and strengthening alumni ties with WBS. The program involved coaching between three and six new MBA students on a no-fee basis, and was offered as a quid pro quo, with no fees payable for the Certificate Program in Leadership Coaching. Upon completion of the training, one would continue to volunteer, and could end up being admitted as a member of the WBS College of Coaches. I excitedly decided to volunteer as I was already mentoring some graduates, and I thought it would be better to do a coaching course.

This turned out to be a correct decision, as you will later read, it became my new passion as I further developed myself, and I am now a certified neuro-linguistic programming practitioner. After a thorough selection process, I was reappointed for the position of Senior Manager Business Development. We intended to appoint more resources in my department, but all the roles were cancelled. I only had two graduate interns to work with. Unfortunately, my manager's contract was terminated and a new person was appointed in his place. It was an internal appointment.

Negotiating My Way Up While Building Allies

Many studies have found that men negotiate more than women (Helgesen and Goldsmith 2018). As I rose up the ranks and in my new role, I knew that being accountable for negotiating transactions meant I had to sharpen my negotiation skills. What I didn't anticipate was negotiating with parties that had just experienced trauma, were hurting, and were angry at the company. My new manager was very open and well experienced in corporate finance and commercial transactions. As a matter of fact, I learned a lot from him and am forever grateful for the depth of knowledge I acquired in structuring mining deals.

We had a great rapport with my boss, who was selfless with his knowledge and supported me in my transaction work. We openly discussed expectations and how we would work. His values and mine were aligned, which made it easier. He was a most effective leader, to the point that when he bought his villa in the middle of Italy, we actually visited him and were his first guests. He supported me in every single way. He was honest and transparent about everything, and I enjoyed working for him. I respect smart bosses as I value strategic thinking and high conceptual skill in a leader. I was impressed and happy with our working relationship. He assigned me the most difficult part of the transactions but he was there to provide guidance and was still leading all three major transactions.

Creating Shared Value for All: The Shared Value Concept

There were three critical transactions that needed to be sealed before December 2014. We were already in February 2013. For many who have been involved in transactions in mining, you would know that a big transaction—in particular a BEE equity transaction—can take up to five years if there are many approvals required. I remember presenting the shared value concept paper, by Porter and Kramer (2011), during the strategy session. What is the shared value concept? The concept of shared value can be defined as policies and operating practices that enhance the competitiveness of a company while simultaneously advancing the economic and social conditions in the communities in which it operates (Porter and Kramer 2011). Shared value creation focusses on identifying and expanding the connections between societal and economic progress. Sustainability and ESG is exactly what this is all about.

The first transaction I successfully negotiated involved the community waiving their statutory right to receive royalties from the company, in exchange for a lump sum cash royalty payment, payable to the company subsidiary, and which would be used by the community to subscribe for shares in the company. The second part was a deferred royalty payment over five years, following completion of the transaction, to be used by the community to pay the administrative costs of running, controlling and directing the affairs of the community. All in all, the community got 3.9% equity in the holding company. The third transaction was the establishment of a Community Trust with an equity stake in the operating asset of the company. The community now holds shares in one of the most progressive mining companies in the world, which is diversified globally. It may have lost value when the previous company's shares took a dive, but ultimately, either way, the company was going to lose.

It goes without saying that such a huge transaction cannot be successfully executed by one person; ultimately, there are one or two people who, if the ball is dropped, would be fired. That was me and my corporate affairs counterparts. The power of the team cannot be overstated. A high-performance team working in a trusting environment produces better results and is stronger than an individual. A team that works together will outperform those that don't. When a new CEO, Ben Magara was appointed, he was smart enough to bring on board a great corporate affairs executive vice president, Lerato Molebatsi, who, I would say, played a huge role in ensuring the deal was sealed. She has such positive energy, which we so needed and was critical. My boss was on leave when I negotiated the transaction with a team from corporate affairs. We worked day and night, engaging community leaders to government officials, to get buy-in and educate them about the transaction and why it was important.

When we started this transaction that involved communities, there was one sceptical person, the head of Legal, who had been assigned to do these transactions with the communities for years and nothing had transpired. But sometimes timing is all it takes, and maybe new leadership. I had a belief it would happen. Sometimes when we face challenges, we need to have a strong mindset of positive belief. Indeed, the first positive step was setting up a meeting with Lerato. No transaction is perfect, but the main goal was achieved. I relentlessly worked day and night, ensuring I held the teams accountable, including our advisors, and not letting things slip. In a deal, there are always key people who follow through all the time and are a constant until a deal is done. At one time, the transaction had a minor problem, and two people ultimately were held accountable to fix it and write a board note, and that included me.

There was one hurdle to overcome: We still had another huge, difficult second transaction. It was the most difficult to negotiate—not only because of the counterparty, but there was a strike that lasted for six months across the platinum industry, and nothing could be done further to negotiate. Then something else happened that almost dampened my spirit. One of the critical senior members from HR, who had relationships with the negotiating party (the representative of employees and unions), and with whom I had started working well together, resigned. I was devastated. I had built a great relationship with him. The deal was in trouble. I was the only constant. I had to make this work and I was running out of time.

The good news was that we had already completed the transaction principles and negotiating framework, but we hadn't started any negotiation. Bear in mind, these were the same employee representatives who had gone through the trauma. It was tough. Nonetheless, we delivered. I worked with advisors to ensure we had covered everything. Negotiating when emotions are high is not an easy task. I was the only one who looked like me in the room full of men. But this is where I learned the power of relationships. I was working like my life depended on this, building rapport and ensuring I didn't lose focus.

Being the only female, you know your job depends on relationships. If you don't, you are doomed; if you do, all is well. Negotiating with the AMCU and other unions was challenging, but where there is the biggest challenge, there is the biggest growth. I learned a lot from this transaction. What I quickly picked up was the power of getting to know the people I was negotiating with. Creating a space where they felt heard was super important as this enabled us to build rapport.

The blueprint for effective negotiation is relationships and having a strategy. Know what you want, but most importantly what your client desires, rather than sticking your head in the sand. Know what levers to use. Know their desire, so that you know what to work with, to ensure alignment and to know how far apart each is from the other's position. A well-thought-through explanation of why you deserve better, based on what their desires are, with clear examples, will win the case. Anyway, you learn the important things to say and what not to say.

Eventually, just a few weeks before the deadline, in December 2014, the deal was finally executed with all approvals. It involved setting up the company Employees Share Ownership Trust (the EST), with the trust acquiring 3.8% of the ordinary share capital of asset. This has seen employees being entitled to share in 3.8% of the profits of the operating asset. No such employee share plan existed before. This is truly the shared value concept as described earlier. We managed to successfully complete all transactions to ensure the company retained its mining licence to operate. This was a huge and important milestone for the previously London listed company.

I took leave then, as I was exhausted and needed a break. I went to visit my sister, Fadzai Chikwava in Saudi Arabia, where she was staying with her family and working as a researcher at KAUST (King Abdullah University of Science and Technology), and her husband Brian Chikwava was working for Aramco. It was a great experience. I was impressed by the advancement of this university when it came to science and technology.

My other prime responsibility was to develop a pipeline of potential opportunities for M&A and other commercial transactions. The company was in the midst of a financial crisis, with cash being preserved, as the company was bleeding cash. There were all these debt covenants that could not be breached. It became an internal business development to ensure we filled the processing capacities in order to remain cash positive. Based on analysts' forecasts, I knew the company was facing huge challenges. I had a son that I needed to pay fees for. I had to make this work. You realise that no one knows the difficulties or challenges you face.

When you present a final board or Exco paper, leaders want to see a positive outcome. You and the people in your team are the ones who know the challenges, and it is up to you to communicate any risks timeously, and to be a problem solver. You are expected to work till late, especially during transactions, and to work relentlessly to ensure you get a positive outcome. There is always someone hungrier who has more to lose, and that was me. I knew if I didn't get this done, I could lose my job. Someone could argue and say that's why you are paid, and fair enough, but how about when it comes to promotion? No one had done this kind of transaction.

When Women Support Each Other, More Women Succeed

The painful but real truth of one barrier to women's advancement, is women already in power. My view with this is that women sabotaging other women is detrimental to closing the gender gap. I have personally experienced only one example in my entire career, and that was in my later career. In all the roles in which I have worked, the females I worked with were very supportive and vice versa, just as at Anglo American. Overall, I have seen and witnessed how women supporting each other can amplify the success of other women. The major difference is that when women support each other more, more is achieved. Hence why I have a strong desire to help women get promoted in their careers.

An example of women supporting women in my career occurred one time when I was presenting. There were only six women out of the 100 top leaders of this company present. I had developed business development themes in collaboration with internal strategy teams, and had provided real-time industry feedback to refine strategy. I had nicely prepared what I believed were the major trends and priorities for the business. There was a sisterhood that was not spoken, but the energy was *you have my back*. I remember recommending geographic and product diversification to the company, such as investing in assets with high palladium content. I thought I did very well, but the feedback I got was not what I expected. 'We have great assets and these strategies don't make sense.' I lost my confidence. The only people who said *Well done* were, of course the females in that room. Again, this is why we need more females in leadership roles.

After the successful delivery of all transactions, my manager's role became available as my manager had resigned. I had high hopes that I would get the position and be promoted. When the role was advertised,

I applied, as that is the logical way. The leader, John, called me to discuss it. He was a very open and straight-talking person. He said he understood I wanted this role, but he didn't believe I was ready. John was not going to promote me despite my delivering on the important social licence to operate. It was not what I expected. I was ready. In my mind, I knew I deserved it, and it hurt. Why then did I sacrifice my relationship, my time, and work so hard? I believed great work spoke for itself. I had never wanted to bring up my successes whenever someone said good things. I thought, *Why should I bother to convince him of my achievements, surely he already knows? If I had done an outstanding job, he surely should have noticed.* I was writing Exco and board papers… I presented updates several times… I was co-ordinating the strategy off-site. Surely, he knows.

The story I had in my mind, consciously and unconsciously at that time was, *I have been overlooked because I am a female.* I had spoken to him because I thought I had met most of the requirements. It is a fair process, which in many cases is followed diligently by companies, however, there is always a thin line. If someone already discounts you that you are not suitable, it makes it difficult.

There are many cases of women, and even men, being overlooked for promotions. People will ask where the data and the evidence is. Most women will quietly leave and go elsewhere, where their skills are utilised. I had heard the expression, *Never fight a company; they have all the financial resources to destroy you*, and it's true especially in the mining industry where the boys club thrives. Many women think about their families, their children, and they ask themselves if it is worth the stress. In many cases, you end up fighting a losing battle as each and every step will have many stresses. You need to have a strong lawyer who can fight for your case, or else you waste time and resources, and needless to say, your brand and reputation is destroyed.

I had a wake-up call when John spoke to me about not promoting me. John clearly had no clue what it took for us to get that licence. What leaders see are the results, and maybe he thought it was a walk in the park. Or maybe he thought advisors did everything, including negotiating with the unions and the community. I felt betrayed. After the incident, given the chance to shine a light on my work, I now don't have any problem speaking for myself. I asked why he believed I was not ready. He mentioned that I didn't have global experience, and he wanted someone with global experience, someone who had worked overseas, especially in capital raising markets. Fair enough.

As I didn't have that experience, and considering the context at the time, where capital for the organisation to survive was paramount, I understood and accepted that. Then he indicated he would appoint externally. I agreed but on one condition: that I would get help with my development and exposure to the global markets to close the gap for future senior roles. I was not going to give up. He didn't refuse, so we agreed. I subsequently made an application for further development as a global leader and experiential plan. Most global organisations have talent pipelines and mapping. Ideally, it should have been in the succession plans.

Unconscious biases are real, and manifest in different kinds of ways. I thought I had worked twice as hard, and felt overlooked for promotion despite delivering, which was a blow to my confidence. As a woman—and worse off, a black woman—it dawned on me that being promoted takes time and a sponsor. Some of the challenges are to have a seat at the table. You lean in but are told you are not ready. I was used to being the only woman, and being the only black woman in my workplace. When you are the only one in the room who looks like you, it takes having more women like you to get promoted. As a high achieving woman, I had to fight to maintain my confidence, and remind myself why I deserved a seat at the big table.

I went through the interview nonetheless, for the position and assessments. There were positive results. They interviewed other people and found someone. In the meantime, I was pursuing the global experience as part of the development that I was told I needed. Bear in mind, all along I was doing both my work and the work of the head of business development, as there was no-one in that role for four months. Knowing your worth is important. It's a guiding light that makes you move forward. I soon learned how to become a more effective advocate for myself and for my team.

I became dissatisfied as I felt unappreciated, and I started to resent my manager and the entire Exco, who obviously didn't seem to be aware of all the hard work I did, delivering on what was one of the most important transactions for the organisation.

Eventually, the company employed Rob, the new head of business development. Needless to say, he indeed had all global credentials, but there was not much difference in terms of BEE transactions. He was a very nice guy and approachable. Bear in mind, I was the only constant. He was my third manager in less than three years. We talked and we scheduled our weekly meetings, and all seemed good. I felt my experience was far more than his as we progressed, but nonetheless, a leader doesn't have to be the expert, right? Wrong! One day as we were having a meeting, he said to me as we were planning our activities for the year, 'Oh, I won't be here for the entire month.' I thought I had heard wrong.

We moved to the following months and it turned out that he was going to be away for a full month, three to four times in a year, and then the following year, he was going to take four to six months to participate in some sports competition. I was shocked. Who was going to be doing the work in his absence? Poor Patience, of course. I was livid. I asked him if his boss knew about this. He said, 'Oh yes, this is what I negotiated before I accepted the offer.' Wow! My heart stopped for a second. He negotiated to be away for almost six or so months in the two years. I was stunned. The anger slowly disappeared. I asked to finish early that day. He saw the shock on my face. I was not angry with him. I was angry with myself. In fact I admired him and thought, *I am such a fool.*

Valuing yourself and knowing your standards and boundaries is critical. There are some people who don't have a standard and will accept anything thrown at them. My dad always used to say, 'Stop being a fool; think smart.' I chose to stop being a fool. This was an epiphany moment for me. Thank God it was on a Friday and I had the entire weekend to strategise. As I was driving home in the heavy traffic of Fourways, I kept repeating my dad's message: *Don't be a fool; think smart. Don't be a fool; think smart.* I decided that my dad would resurrect from his grave if I continued working in this organisation in this setting. I thought: *This is my life and I have to be the author of my life, and no one else.*

We had a family Friday ritual of having dinner out. I narrated the story, and they were livid. They asked me what I was going to do. I mumbled something incoherent. I didn't know yet what I was going to do, but what I did know was that I didn't want to continue working there. I needed something. I went to church on Sunday and prayed to God to guide me through the process, as I needed wisdom. Afterwards, I was sitting on the patio, reflecting, and watching nine doves sitting in my pool. A thought came to me, like a lightning flash. I felt a sense of relief. I knew what I needed to do. *Why don't I take sabbatical leave? Go and study.* But how would I pay for my studies and bills. Do I resign? The voice kept giving me ideas. *You need development. Remember, that's why you were not promoted.* Yes, I knew exactly what I needed to do.

On Monday, as if he had read my mind, my boss came in with a letter. It was an increase in my salary. Oh, I had recently received my yearly increase. What is this for? To thank me for the work I did. I was grateful, and I signed it and smiled. We had an honest conversation. He mentioned that he understood my situation in that I hadn't been promoted for his role, and that he would like to help in any way. I said yes, I needed his help. I wanted to go to Insead as part of my development plan. I had researched the executive programs I needed. Insead was one that struck me. I was going to do an AMP and the deadline was very close. I immediately applied and asked my new boss to endorse it, which he did. As the saying goes: strike while the iron's still hot. He was happy to support me.

My application to Insead was accepted. I was happy. I hadn't taken my long leave for a while and I had a credit of more than 60 days owing. I decided to take leave from June to the end of August, including study leave. That was effectively almost four months. I needed the break. As all this was happening, the company's financial performance was further deteriorating. I was approached by another mining company. It was new and I didn't know it that well but the role sounded amazing. I attended the interviews and my-self talk then was: *I am leaving my employer. I am done. I am not the person who should be here. I should be a white, tall male, not this tiny black woman. This is not for me.* I blamed myself. Why did I even get to this situation? For the first time, I paid for an executive coach. I thought maybe there was something wrong with me.

On June 5, 2015, I was on my flight to Europe, where I was setting out to travel across eight countries. For the first time, I didn't read anything. I reflected on my journey. As the pilot announced our departure to London, I was filled with gratitude for how just one small decision had changed the entire course of my life and career. I was on my way to Insead. I would be meeting interesting people and learning new things. To top it off, I had received an offer from my new employer to pay for my studies. This time, I was a tough negotiator. I negotiated hard, as I had learned from Rob.

I think I have possibly read every self-help book to continue in my quest to improve my confidence, and I listen to inspirational podcasts while driving. I have also performed positive affirmations. C-Suite executive women in STEM are sometimes seen as being too ambitious, and once others see this, you can be a victim of bullying, which is intended to bring you down. Sometimes I don't understand the meaning of *too ambitious*. As you will see in this chapter, for me, the priority is to continuously deliver above expectations. Working with people who support you, particularly female leaders, is the mechanism to succeeding. But it also starts with having a strategy for your career, and knowing what you want.

Having confidence and the courage to ask those uncomfortable questions is something I found I had to do. If you read too much and overthink about what people will think, you end up second-guessing yourself and not asking the questions you want to ask. It's a technique I developed over time. The more you do it, the more you become unconsciously skilled. But there is always a catch. The question is, how strong are your self-limiting belief systems? With me, that voice that kept saying *you are not good enough* was a self-limiting belief system that was not at a conscious level at that point in my career. I was not aware of it by then, as I had succeeded tremendously over the years and didn't have many doubts. But it only takes one traumatic incident to trigger that unconscious limiting belief system.

I kept thinking, *I will work even harder, with consistency and resilience, as I have done before.* But I soon realised I was being hard on myself. I had an *aha* moment when I realised the behaviours that helped me get where I was could also hold me back from advancing to the next stage. I spent too much energy trying to be perfect, trying to please, or overvaluing expertise, at the expense of relationships and in being me. I was hoping to be spontaneously noticed and rewarded for my hard work, instead of advocating for myself for my promotion. My focus was on demonstrating loyalty to the company by delivering. Lessons learnt.

INSEAD Experience: No One Will Give You Permission to Succeed: Own Your Success

France is known for its fashion houses, classical art museums—including the Louvre—and heritage sights and monuments such as the Eiffel Tower. This was my third time in Paris. Insead is one of the world's leading and largest graduate business schools, offering a truly global educational experience. The Insead Europe Campus is nestled in the vast forest of Fontainebleau.

Developing friendships and networks is critical for your career. When I chose Insead, I was looking for something that was different, and to meet great people. Insead was a marvellous experience. I arrived in Paris three days before the program started, so I had enough time to relax after a long trip around Europe. I went and did what every woman does when they arrive in Paris: shopping. It's a shopper's paradise. What made this amazing was that there were mad sales. I was buying clothes as cheaply as $10, and meeting interesting people.

The quality of the course materials and the lecturers were great. I knew the things I needed to develop myself: Negotiation was one of those, and presenting in front of many people was second. Based on interview results, I thought I needed better communication skills. We were put in groups of eight or so. The cases I enjoyed the most were about Margaret Thatcher and Chris Johnson, a Nestle CEO. The Chris Johnson case stood out more. We were tasked to analyse the case and to prepare a possible presentation for Chris when he had to address disgruntled senior members at the conference. My team selected me to do the presentation. This was a chance for me to practice what I had learned about communication. I stood there. I looked everyone in the eye, I paused and had that uncomfortable silence. I used the emotion to influence. I used data—I used all I could. All I knew was that I nailed it, mostly because I connected with my audience and had a huge sound of applause. But it turned out that the outcome was not what we presented. For me, that was not the point. I knew I had done a great job. I practised what I had learned, which is the beauty of attending a world-class business school like Insead. I received a job offer from a global Australian mining company while I was at Insead. At the same time, I and other employees were all asked to apply for voluntary separation at the current company, as it was near bankruptcy.

Prior to the Insead experience, I had travelled to over ten countries in Europe and really enjoyed it. I had visited Amsterdam; Germany; the Rhine Falls and Lucerne in Switzerland; Innsbruck in Austria; Venice and Rome in Italy, where I was amazed at the Pantheon, the Roman Forum and St Peters basilica. Then I was back in Paris, ready for the Insead experience. We then spent another three weeks travelling the Loire Valley. We visited nearly all the chateaux, from Chambord, Chaumont Sur Loire, and Cheverny. My favourite was Chenonceau. Travelling is a wonderful part of life, and the best way to get away from a busy schedule, and is a good remedy for stress, anxiety and depression as the brain builds new neurons, so I have been told! Travelling is all about exploring new places, cultures, cuisines, rituals and styles of living. It's what I needed in order to realise there was more to life than just work.

At the end of the day, I turned my pain into growth. Had I not met Rob and experienced feeling overlooked for promotion, I wouldn't have grown. In hindsight, he probably deserved the position more than

I. Why? Because he must have impressed the boss for him to have conceded and given him that awesome deal to be away for almost six or so months on the same salary. I sincerely admired him and knew: *That is what I call knowing exactly what you want, how to get it, and not being apologetic.* Ultimately, I was able to quickly learn, and turned the situation around so as not to be a victim but to ask myself, what is the learning here?

Sometimes we look at situations as if we have been unfairly treated, but are there some behaviours we are not aware of that may be barriers to our advancement? Or is it the boys' club playing out as Rob had a glass cushion? This was the beginning of understanding what a boys' club is, and the unconscious biases that exist. I don't doubt that the boss genuinely was concerned about the company and looked at his decision purely from a point of managing risk, and he did not necessarily fail to appoint me because I was a black female. It was a typical case of unconscious bias. At that point in my career, I chose the former, for the learning and development I needed. Consequently, I was attending the Insead Business School rather than believing there is a glass cushion that exists in male-dominated workplaces. But as you read this book, you will see the boys' club playing out even more as you rise.

Exercise

Whether it's in business or in our personal life, we are constantly negotiating. We sometimes under-estimate the power of negotiating and getting what we want as female leaders. My epiphany moment was with Rob. In my view, he made me change my story from being a victim to being victorious. Negotiation is one of the most critical skills required to succeed in a male-dominated workplace.

You can download a free negotiation template from
www.unleashingmysuperpowers.com/bonuses.

CHAPTER 7

BOUNCING BACK
WITH THE HELP OF A COACH

You can tell whether a man is clever by his answers.
You can tell whether a man is wise by his questions.
– Naguib Mahfouz, Winner of the 1988 Nobel Prize for Literature

Mentoring and Coaching

When I volunteered to be a leadership coach for MBA students at Wits Business School, I had no idea I was going to continue to coach until I turned it into a profession. I signed up for coaching to impact and help the MBA students in their leadership journey. I found it fulfilling. Not only did I learn about the challenges these leaders were experiencing in their lives, and the impact I was making in their career progression, but I also developed my listening skills and guided them without judgement. It became my calling. I completed the first year and received my certificate for leadership coaching in 2014. I continued volunteering for the love and passion of it, and now it has been close to seven years since I started. When you do what you love, it's not work.

Since coaching is the difference between introspection and reflection, it can help you to understand and discover your purpose in life. The question around purpose has shaped who I want to be in life. I now feel I am more in touch with my calling, and as a consequence of this knowledge, I have started shaping my career around my purpose to use my unique talents to serve others. I took the next step towards the bigger picture of fulfilling my purpose in life through establishing Peak Performance with Patience, a leadership and executive coaching company to help women navigate the male-dominated workplace, in the corporate world and as entrepreneurs: making a difference.

Women do need mentors, but most importantly, they need coaches too. In these modern days of technology, I think women can make use of what I call a tribe of supporters. The playing field is not even, as several studies have shown. More men have sponsors rather than mentors, in male-dominated workplaces. This is explained more under the topic of the boys' club, especially in the mining industry. The interviews we conducted as part of a campaign of what it takes to achieve in STEM and leadership, showed that we do need men to mentor the women, and not women alone in male-dominated workplaces. In addition, you need a coach who will help you when you get stuck. Mentorship has been proven to be essential, especially for graduates to mid-career level. Mentorship and sponsorship have become a crucial element for career advancement and have grown over the years, especially for women who want to break the C-Suite glass ceiling. Sponsorship, which is not so common. The question is not whether sponsorship is good or bad, but it's about levelling the playing field for a black woman, as it has been shown white males are likely to sponsor younger white males or white females. If an organisation does not have a transparent talent management program, and ensure they formalise mentorship programs, then it becomes unfair for black women.

How then does a woman working in a predominantly male workplace request someone to be a sponsor? This is a question I am normally asked by younger women I coach. My answer is always that having to build strong relationships first is important. The next is ensuring there is a natural professional connection, and this normally comes from having your manager as your mentor or sponsor. I've been lucky to have mentors and sponsors most of my career life. Many are informal people that I connected with in the mining industry. But I was also fortunate to have my two sisters as my mentors, and then having my bosses and some of the people that I worked with to bounce ideas off.

Substituting new belief systems for old ones is empowering, and it's also something one can do with the help of a coach. I had a coach who helped me to overcome some limiting belief systems that became habits or patterns that were actually not aspects of my character. The first time I had an executive coach was in my last role, when I was overlooked for a promotion. Before I attended Insead Business School, I scheduled my first session with him as I didn't know how to deal with the fact that I had been overlooked, or rather, felt I worked hard enough and deserved a promotion. Interestingly, he was a white male. I wanted some honest feedback and not sympathy or anything resembling it. He turned out to be the best coach ever.

What I liked about his coaching was the way he asked incisive questions about what exactly I wanted in my career. He wanted me to be clear about what my values were and what I thought success would look like. But most importantly, he wanted to know how I gave meaning to my experiences. He helped me see the experience that I had, as an opportunity for growth. He kept asking and re-framing, 'What does this experience mean for you? Why do you think the boss has indeed overlooked you? Have you had any problems with him before?' I answered *No*. 'Does he treat you differently to others of the same gender and sex?' Again, I was able to answer *No*, but what I knew was that he respected more people with a finance background. My coach was trying to make me see the situation differently and to help me see this particular experience differently.

I had grown accustomed to these behaviours as a way to cope with stress and in trying to fit into a world that was never designed for a corporate black woman. Old habits take time to change into new habits, as studies have shown. My old habits had been repeated and repeated, and over time they became unconscious. With time, I became unconsciously competent. I got into the habit of asking better questions, or rather challenging my assumptions. My coach told me that by saying *Yes*, even when that answer did not really serve my interests, I was the one who put myself in a difficult position. This is because I am a people pleaser. I was the only one with the power to change that. To get unstuck and to let go of a behaviour that was no longer serving me, I needed to first of all recognise it as a habit and bring it to conscious awareness. Doing so helped me to unleash energy and confidence, and that energy made me feel alive again. I could not have seen that without my coach's honest feedback.

I was able to redefine the problem in solvable terms. What was also profound was when my coach mentioned, 'Focus on what you can solve that is within your control, and have clarity on what makes you happy. How will you know when you see it? How will you feel?' Those few sessions were powerful. I started asking myself what I could do to change my situation in order to get where I wanted to be. That was the day I saw the nine doves and, *boom*, there was my answer. This is how I ended up making my way to Insead and changing my story. Not only did my new employer pay for my studies, but I also had the best experience at Insead, and that propelled my career.

I would always seek general guidance from many people who supported me in my career, such as discussing specific opportunities that they could offer. Mentorship is supposed to be more of a reciprocal nature than it may appear. Sociologists and psychologists have long observed our deep desire to participate in reciprocal behaviour. That humans feel obligated to return favours has been documented in virtually all societies, and underpins all kinds of social relationships. The mentor/mentee relationship is no exception. Done right, everybody flourishes.

The concept of mentorship and coaching is often confused by many. This is why I started the group coaching sessions and mentorship program to help women in male-dominated workplaces. In the digital era, one can have a wide selection of mentors to choose from. Some things to avoid when engaging a mentor in my experience is using a mentor as a psychologist for all personal problems. Yes, there are occasions when a mentee wants to "download" all their problems to the mentor. But limit this to career related problems and rather seek a psychologist and rather focus more on specific problems where you need guidance on real solutions. Mentors walk with you on your journey and can help in problem solving. Sometimes it can be difficult to ask for help but asking for support is not a sign of weakness and is often the first step to finding a path forward.

Coaching relationships often form between individuals who have a common interest. Boundaries and rules of coaching should be set up-front. There is a difference between coaching and mentoring: Coaching: I walk alongside you; mentoring: I put you on my back, and I walk while you learn how I walk.

In the male-dominated workplace, there are many men in leadership positions, especially in the mining industry. This is where the boys' club starts and continues to flourish. Even though progress has been made in getting more female leaders in leadership roles, it is still not enough. Therefore, women are still left behind, making it impossible for the less experienced women to get enough support, unless male champions take the lead. For example, in my case, there were very few females in my time, and had it not been for the male champions who were my sponsors, I wouldn't have been recognised in my career. The call to action, to male champions of diversity and inclusion, has been made through forums, but the progress is very slow. Take for example in Chapter 8, where we show statistics of top female leaders in the mining industry.

Junior women avoid engaging in mentoring relationships with senior men because of fear of what people may think. This is why we need more females in leadership positions, because of the same issue of fear of what people may think. How then do females progress in male-dominated workplaces and be promoted if this is one of the barriers? We have shown that having a sponsor is what it takes for females, and this gets even stronger as you rise to C-Suite. How does a black, smart female then connect with a white, older male without feeling as though she is dating him? Let's get more females in positions of influence, C-Suite and board. As much as companies can have policies to help remove such stigmas, we need more formal processes to level the playing field. Why should I go and play golf when I don't feel like playing golf and I have children to take care of? Incentives within the company policy should be part of this. Who are you coaching and mentoring?

The second issue is, we need wide, industry-led, formal mentorship sponsorship programs, as these have been shown to be successful in other industries. The third proposal is having formal coaching programs for men, on how to be effective mentors for women. I like the Accenture model, where a junior staff member is assigned a career counsellor. Not many companies have this model. This helps women navigate the work environment of a male-dominated workplace. My view is that what is needed is executive leadership development programs that are targeted at senior women across the industry, who are approaching promotion to C-Suite. They should have an executive coach and a sponsor, and they should shadow members of the executive committee and have a global assignment. There should be a timeline for completion. Many companies, such as Anglo American, have such programs.

Striving for Excellence in Everything You Do is Key

My personal and professional background and skills are diverse and interesting. In everything I do, I strive for outstanding results. When I returned from the four-month long trip at Insead in Europe, I was full of energy. I was excited to be back, as I had a new job offer with a fairly new organisation. Because I had two coaches: a female coach from Insead and my executive coach—a white male—it made my transition and settling into my new role much easier.

My role as Regional Commercial Manager for Africa was to lead the commercial function after the aggregation of the four operating assets, as the company had just demerged from the big company and had a separate listing. This included building the commercial and business development strategy to align with the overall regional strategy, with oversight of its implementation, and then leading a multidisciplinary team (internal and external) to generate potential opportunities and analysis to influence the outcome of divestments and acquisitions activities. The role was a consolidation of all my 15 years' experience in metallurgy, strategy and business development. It was challenging but very exciting. Each day was filled with new challenges and transactions that I was excited to deliver.

As you become a functional head, how you spend your time becomes more important. I consider myself someone who has been able to build great relationships with my bosses and co-workers. This role stretched me beyond being just a manager, and in spending more time setting and communicating strategy for the function in the context of the business strategy. Managing upwards and horizontally became more important, and not just with my team. The success of the role was based on the ability to detect dangers and opportunities before they arose. I had to make some tough decisions, like letting go of some of my team members. To thrive and succeed in this role also required the support of my leader, who empowered me to make decisions and lead the team.

When your values and the values of the person you report to, or those who lead, are aligned, it makes your life easier to lead and deliver. Coaching skills became even more relevant, not only in developing the team but in working with a multidisciplinary team in executing transactions. Managing a complex network of relationships within the business, and with a corporate development team and the regional Exco, was critical, and this is where the Insead Development Program assisted me with those skills. I also do take pride in my connectedness, and I see it as an essential aspect of the value I provide.

While I was having the courage and vision to radically reshape the function to create value, we had a restructuring process. This resulted in the commercial function being elevated to Exco. In the process, I was in receipt of good news: I was promoted to vice president after delivering various transactions in a short space of time and establishing the commercial function. The eight months I spent in this role stretched my leadership skills, which was about leading others: from influencing, to negotiation, to leading teams to deliver.

This shows how, in less than a year, I had a career setback but decidedly rebounded—rather than getting stuck in grief and blame—I explored how I contributed to what went wrong, I evaluated whether I had sized up the situation correctly and reacted appropriately. What I didn't mention was that at Insead, we had to do a 360-degree assessment. What this entailed was getting 12 to 17 people to provide feedback on our leadership competencies. I went back to my previous employer and requested honest feedback. That feedback gave me some new insights on some of my blind spots and weaknesses. One of the responses I was given was that I was spending too much time with my teams and co-workers, and not enough time managing upwards. But most importantly, the feedback highlighted some of what I call my superpowers—which are my strengths. I had a development plan to work on my challenges and was slowly making progress when I started in my new role at this new company. Having that willingness to learn from my missteps was the first step in becoming a better leader.

A metaphor on the learnings that the actions of buffalos bring to great leaders is how they react during storms. When faced with an oncoming storm, buffalos run into it, thereby minimizing their exposure to its impact. For great leaders, it is all about *how* great leaders choose to address their professional or personal storms: avoid them and run away, or confront and deal with them. Are you a buffalo? Be that mighty buffalo who courageously confronts the storm, finds learning in running (and dancing) in the rain, and enjoys the beautiful sunshine and rainbows that follow.

Leading oneself, then others, and then business, is critical to unleashing your superpowers. It all starts with leading self, and having the courage to request feedback, and learning from it to move forward. Knowing what drives you is particularly important. I am driven by a relentless quest to make an impact. I strongly feel connected with an organisation when I feel that the company is benefitting from my analytical thinking, my leadership, my resourcefulness and problem-solving skills.

Considering the career changes I have made, I am often asked by my clients about my transition into these various roles. I answer that a transition from a STEM specialist to either strategy or planning, or even to business development, is not difficult. My experience has shown that if you have a STEM background, you are likely to have strong conceptual and analytical skills. There are obviously other skills that play a role in success, including negotiation, communication, and influencing, that one needs to learn. Another important component is knowing what you are passionate about. At each point in my career, I have been, and am still passionate about developing strategies for companies. I know that all my strengths are being utilised and I enjoy each challenge and the sense that every day is different.

As a leader, do you know your challenges and your superpowers?

Patience at Insead Business School, Paris, in July 2015

Exercise

You are a leader of an organisation and you have people that report to you. Knowing oneself is the first step to being the greatest leader.

What do you think your direct reports would say about your leadership style? What are four words and sentences that they would use to describe you? Write these down.

CHAPTER 8

FROM BOYS' CLUB
TO MALE CHAMPIONS:
THE ROLE OF ESG

The time is always right to do what is right.
– Martin Luther King Junior

When You Find Your Purpose:
My Role as Vice President for Sustainability

"This is very good work. I really like the work that Dr. Mpofu is doing." I didn't know what to say when the minister said this about me to my former boss. This was just before the minister gave her keynote speech. After several attempts to get a high-profile figure, we managed to get at least three leaders who are advocates for gender, diversity and inclusion. We closed off the meeting for the event to start, as everyone was waiting for her entrance.

Diversity and inclusion were the hot topics discussed in front of over 300 CEOs, government officials and NGOs at the event I organised when I was appointed to the role of sustainability, as Vice President Corporate Affairs Africa, for a global mining company. I was happy with my job and good at closing deals in mergers and acquisitions. Eight months into my commercial role, I was promoted to vice president in a role that was completely new to me. I had no idea I was going to find my purpose.

My role was multifaceted, stimulating and fulfilling. I have since become a thought leader in sustainability in the mining industry, speaking at various international conferences. This only happened because male champions of diversity and inclusion said, "Yes, she can do this job." When a leader allows you to thrive in the role and stretches you with challenges, you feel empowered to do more. At no point in this role did I feel disempowered. Likewise, I did the same for my team, as one of my 360-degree feedbacks was that I am an empowering leader. For that I am forever grateful to my former boss.

This role closely aligned with my desire to make an impact. Our organisation's mission was to make a difference for generations to come. I was connected to our mission statement and lived up to it. Leadership is about influence and using your voice, and my new role created a platform that allowed me to do that. I was responsible for leading and overseeing the development, execution and reporting of sustainability (aligned with the UN SDG), risks, mitigation and issues management, to protect the company from reputational risk and to align with ESG requirements. In addition, I was responsible for driving the socio-economic development of the company's mining areas, while maintaining company stakeholder and community engagement strategies.

This role exposed me to a different level of leadership, with a lot of lobbying and external affairs. I represented the company in important leadership forums and memberships of various industry bodies, lobbying and advocating to influence policy. In 2017 and 2018, my boss and I attended the prestigious Ministerial Symposium, which brings together more than 100 C-level mining executives and government officials, including ministers and vice ministers of mining and energy, and mining company CEOs prior to the Mining Indaba. The Africa Mining Vision (AMV) is a platform focussed on creating an inclusive and sustainable mining sector across Africa, as well as elevating the industry by tracking achievements and better communicating the important contribution of mining to the economic development of societies.

The Mining Indaba is a well-known platform where the entire mining industry network meets yearly and thought leaders from investment banks to mining leaders speak. We sponsored a luncheon to discuss diversity and inclusion at this forum. This was my first official event. It was the first ever Women in Mining luncheon that we co-sponsored, and it was not only well attended—with over 300 government, NGOs and industry influencers—but we also had the honourable ministers.

All genders attended the luncheon and were committed to solving the gender and inclusion issues that impact the industry. Platforms like these that seek to make a difference in the industry are essential. That year, the executive director for UN Women invited me to be a member of the Global Innovation Coalition for Change (GICC) to advance women and girls in STEM.

Patience speaking at the
Mining Indaba Conference on ESG in mining

I was reluctant to claim my achievements. Over the years, I have gone the extra mile with every project I worked on to deliver high-quality work. For example, when I led the commercial team for the Africa region, I took on every little commercial project. I never said *no*. I enjoyed the work, so it was not work for me. The people I worked with were super smart. My boss supported me and never doubted my capabilities. I excelled. The beauty of a commercial role is that you can easily quantify your performance by its results.

A stakeholder and corporate affairs role, on the other hand, is subjective. It's one of the most underrated roles and yet one of the most important. Relationship-building is the foundation of the role, which is essential at levels 5–7 (strategic roles, C-Suite and above). At the same time, being in that role means you must sometimes be the bearer of bad news, as my buddy used to say. Sometimes I had to be creative and reframe the bad news as something positive, without sugar-coating the risks to the organisation.

When we went through significant restructuring that severely impacted my role and division, I was the only woman with no role at the VP level. I felt betrayed and disappointed. I had worked so hard—most of the time, harder than my male peers, so I felt. I was the first into the office each day and the last to leave, often working weekends. I considered the prospects of being unemployed: I still had huge debts in property investments and I was taking a voluntary separation. I was going through my second separation, and being a single mother made it difficult. I had hit rock bottom in my career.

Sometimes talent is wasted by not having a supportive culture. I found myself banging on a solid rock sometimes, as I felt unsupported by some of my peers. My spirit was drained. I had become someone I didn't like. I had always considered myself someone who built great relationships with co-workers. My manager used to say that everything was going well. I was stunned when, during my annual performance review, my leader said I needed to do more on stakeholders' engagement.

I couldn't believe it, considering the context. It was easy to forget that I had no handover and I had never worked in the role. Seven roles in that department were vacant when I took over, with low morale. Having my efforts and skills go unacknowledged made me feel unseen and undervalued. How could he not recognise what I had contributed? I built the team from scratch, engaged government and communities, reduced community unrest, rebuilt the company brand, and positioned it as a company that makes a difference. Sometimes it's not about who is right or wrong; it's about acknowledging that people make decisions that make sense for the business at the time. Effective leaders can learn and move forward with new insights. I chose to be the kind of leader who learns and moves forward.

One thing I have mastered over the years is resilience. I quickly realised I am the master of my own destiny and not a victim. As Oprah says, 'Most people suffer and chase a dream that doesn't belong to them'. You can't always get what you want, but you can avoid falling into the trap of the victim mentality. The choices we make can either enhance or drain our spirit. I chose the former. Refusing to be a victim has been a source of my strength.

I asked myself how my own behaviour might have contributed to this, and what I could do to change it. In other words, I shifted my attention to what was within my power to fix. This seemed like an example of the glass cliff, but upon further reflection, it's about valuing yourself. That is why my coaching always starts with "Leading Self", which is knowing yourself.

Considering the perspectives of others who may have been going through emotional challenges during the restructuring described earlier made it easier to understand and forgive. Meeting people where they are is important. It takes maturity and spiritual strength to be the leader you are called to be in such situations. I put my energy into identifying what I could control. I have learned never to dwell on negative events, but rather focus on learning from them. When things are out of my control, I tap into the spiritual realm, as I believe in God. Grace gives you courage and strength in the face of adversity.

Research has shown that people's behaviours are altered to meet the expectations of their peer groups. Who you spend your time with is who you become. I always made sure to align my expectations with whomever I worked with. You don't always get to choose your bosses or peers, but when you do, you should base your decision on whether your values are aligned. Your bosses often become your mentors and sponsors, and eventually your champions.

Sometimes events redirect you to your purpose. After this I decided I needed to make changes in my life, but not just externally anymore. My health and family mattered the most to me, and all I wanted was to spend more time with them. A part of me knew there was something deeper I needed to do. I realised I needed this break to reflect. I was fortunate that the company supported my decision to pursue personal growth.

Dr. Patience Mpofu at the UN Women GICC in New York in 2017

Invisible Barriers for Women
in Male-Dominated Workplaces

There are still many invisible barriers that hold women back from advancing in the mining sector. For example, in September 2020, we conducted a survey as part of my legacy project on what it takes to succeed in a male-dominated workplace (STEM). This study looked at women across various industries, but given that I am from mining, 65% were from that industry. Most mining companies now have gender-inclusive policies. The major barriers are invisible, and the industry acknowledges that more needs to be done.

Most of the women we have interviewed are not confident to apply for promotions, even when they deserve them more than their male colleagues, believing that good job performance will naturally be rewarded. Some of the challenges facing women include passive-aggressive behaviours (bullying), being undermined, toxic leadership, systemic racism and exclusion, and a culture that does not support women who speak up or excel at their jobs. Women are rewarded for being obedient and not outshining their bosses. One lady said, 'I truly think the lack of advancement comes from decision-makers choosing to support incompetent people who are vocal about vague achievements. It's the system that needs to change, not only women.' Another, when asked about invisible barriers, enumerated, 'Not being treated equally, coping with aggression and competitiveness, women pulling each other down, pay parity'. Other common complaints were men speaking over women, people claiming credit they don't deserve, and the boss failing to give proper recognition.

One of the points that came up frequently was not having enough women in leadership positions. Carol's case is an example where navigating the boys' club becomes a challenge starting from the recruitment process. This can happen to anyone, male or female. She was a senior executive with more than 25 years' mining experience at C-Suite level. She was headhunted by an executive search firm in London for a role in one of the biggest global mining companies in the world. After going through a series of interviews over the course of eight months—including with the CEO of one of the divisions and four C-Suite executives—and passing the medical and references checks, Carol was declined, despite being promised an offer and even being invited for a strategy session.

To better understand some of the invisible barriers faced by women, we need to understand the history of mining. Most of these barriers stem from the fact that the mining industry was not previously a workplace for females. The mining industry has played a critical role in economic development for over 140 years. Globally, many countries have resources and reserves of major commodities that are used for many functions. The major mining countries include but are not limited to South Africa, Chile, Australia, Brazil, China, Russia, India, Peru, Democratic Republic of Congo, Zimbabwe, Namibia, Botswana, and Canada. After a period of intensive mining, the industry remains a major contributor to most economies, in particular those of South Africa and Australia, making significant contributions to employment numbers and export earnings, as well as attracting foreign direct investment. For example, in 2019, the mining industry in South Africa contributed R361.6 billion to GDP, employing over 451,427 people (Minerals Council of South Africa).

Mining is a labour-intensive industry. Modern mining processes involve prospecting for ore bodies, analysing the profit potential of mines, extracting the desired materials, and reclaiming the land after the mine is closed.

Mineral processing, which was my area of specialisation, is a technical area in the science of metallurgy that studies the mechanical means of crushing, grinding, and washing that enable the separation of valuable metals or minerals from their gangue (waste material). Since most metals are present in ores as oxides or sulfides, the metal needs to be reduced to its metallic form. Miners must adhere to stringent environmental and rehabilitation codes to minimise environmental impact. My PhD involved tailings retreatment. Ore mills generate large amounts of waste, called tailings. Tailings are usually produced as a slurry. For example, 5.3 grams of gold is extracted per ton of ore; a ton of gold produces 200,000 tons of tailings.

Many products would not exist if it weren't for mining. Mined metals are the essential ingredients in smartphones, electric cars and wind turbines, while PGMs are auto catalysts to reduce emissions. Copper and iron are used to build our homes, offices, railways and airports. Cobalt is used in alloys for aircraft engine parts. Copper is used in electrical equipment such as wiring and motors. Lithium is used in rechargeable batteries for mobile phones, laptops, digital cameras and electric vehicles. Mining produces products that move the world towards a more sustainable future. We need to create a new narrative, especially in Africa where most people are not aware of the importance of the resources they possess.

Historically, one of the biggest concerns that many women had about working underground was safety. Previous underground conditions lacked toilet and changing facilities for women. The industry has made significant progress in trying to attract more women, particularly with safety. A challenge that many women used to face, including myself, was overalls and personal protective equipment (PPE) that didn't fit properly, being historically designed with men in mind. This is now a thing of the past.

Another concern was physical limitations. In the gold and platinum industries especially, some mines are up to three kilometres deep. These mines were, and still are, labour-intensive, requiring physically arduous work under challenging conditions. In general terms, most women do not have the same levels of physical strength as most men, and this has a material impact on their ability to work underground effectively. Over the past few years, the industry has put considerable effort into making equipment more appropriate for women.

That was the Industrial Age, and now we are in the Digital Economy. Leaders need to consider whether we are asking the right questions about how to remove limitations to get more women to participate. Modernisation is critical. As mining becomes more digital, physical strength and stamina will be replaced by fine motor skills and problem-solving abilities as pre-requisites. These shifts will create significant opportunities for women, especially STEM professionals.

While the industry has made strides in inclusivity, there continue to be invisible barriers that make women reluctant to enter the industry. Key partnership with all stakeholders, including government, and having more female role models in leadership positions is critical. We need to call out organisations and leaders that are not gender inclusive.

The survey we conducted, with 65% of women being from the mining industry, showed that they still face these unseen barriers. The progression of women in top management in the mining industry in

South Africa, where I spent most of my career, from 17% in 2019 to 25%, is a huge step towards achieving gender equality in the sector. There is no doubt the various organisations are committed to gender equality, but progress is slow due to the boys' club culture that still prevails, particularly as one moves into C-Suite and board positions. Take the case study presented where the company, with no explanation, declined to accept Carol, a highly-qualified woman.

The boys' club leaders, who don't listen to women's voices, are the main barriers to women's advancement. The unconscious biases that favour the hiring and promotion of men are real, and continue to play a role in undermining women's advancement. Although there has been some progress over the years, workplace structures and policies are still not designed to be inclusive of women.

Cultures where leadership tolerates the kinds of behaviours that make the workplace exclusive are detrimental to closing the gender gap. External forces, including unconscious bias, subtly penalise women if they raise their voices, labelling them troublesome. Hence why it is important for women to be part of a community of likeminded women to amplify their voices. If workplaces are designed for men, by men, who should be redesigning the new workplaces that are diverse and inclusive? Women! This can only be done if we raise our voices. We cannot wait for life to happen to us.

Sponsorship in the Workplace

A lack of sponsorship is preventing women from advancing, as evidenced by the survey we did. Women are likely to achieve if they have a male sponsor. It's important to have courageous men willing to support women, especially black women. I have had some male champions with great leadership skills. One of them in particular I can't forget, for the legacy he left behind. He was someone with whom I knew where I stood. There were no secrets or playing politics. He had my full commitment. As I reflect on what he stood for, I realise that my values and his were aligned.

Integrity, trust and authenticity go hand in hand, along with giving and receiving feedback. As said previously, your manager becomes your mentor, then becomes your sponsor, and eventually becomes your champion. Building a strong relationship with your leader is the first step towards having someone mention your name when opportunities arise. But again, it's better to have more women in leadership positions who can advocate for younger women.

Navigating the Boys' Club: Glass Ceiling and Glass Cliff

The boys' club has existed for many years, as we read in any history of work and workplaces. Men were the breadwinners and women were the stay-at-home nurturers. Subsequently, men built clubs to enjoy as they rose through the ranks in their careers. In the mining industry, these clubs have evolved to be either a Chamber of Mines or a Minerals Council. No women were allowed at these meetings where a culture of sponsorship and networking was formed. Over time, these clubs have become more inclusive and broader in their missions.

They represent the interests of various companies and now work collaboratively to lobby with various institutions, especially with government, on policy issues. Influence is more powerful if you have a community of likeminded people with one or two missions that tie them together. Historically, the meetings of these associations were where most decisions took place, such as career advancement and promotions. How inclusive are such clubs now? Do women really have a voice?

While we see women as board members of some of these organisations, it's important to increase their representation to ensure that diversity, equity and inclusion are top priorities alongside issues of safety. Working collaboratively with the Women's Associations is critical, to ensure that issues women have raised are dealt with and they are not talked over. It is commendable that Minerals Council South Africa has taken that step and launched Women in Mining Leadership, and work in collaboration with Women in Mining. Only proper female representation at board level is lacking.

The *glass ceiling* is a metaphor used to represent an invisible barrier that keeps a given demographic from rising above a certain level in a hierarchy. The metaphor was created by feminists referring to barriers in the careers of high-achieving women (Sandberg 2013). It also refers to obstacles hindering the advancement of minorities, like black women. Most women across all areas of the workforce are faced with the glass ceiling, especially to enter C-Suite positions. How then do these powerful networks help women break the glass ceiling and avoid the glass cliff?

The glass cliff is when a female leader is appointed to fix things during a crisis. There are many examples of this. During the COVID-19 pandemic, we witnessed how many women rose to the occasion to lead. In the corporate world, most women don't survive the glass cliff. Take Cynthia Carroll, who we discussed earlier, as an example. Cynthia took over in a company that was experiencing safety challenges.

How can leaders ensure that women are appointed based on merit without being set up for failure? One may argue that men are always dealing with companies in a crisis, but if we were to calculate how many women have been appointed in a crisis versus in a normal situation, we would, I'm sure, find that the former is more common.

The Role of ESG in Creating More Female Leaders

ESG in mining has become more important than ever, creating a perfect storm for women to lean in and get promoted. Women occupy less than one-fifth of the leadership roles across global mining companies, according to a new S&P Global Market Intelligence (2020) analysis of executives and board members. Gender diversity has increasingly been a focus for investors; however, women make up just 14.9% of mining companies' executive ranks, 18.1% of the industry's board positions, and 13.2% of the sector's C-Suite executive roles.

Companies that provide an inclusive environment, supporting work-life balance and flexible work arrangements, will eventually gain a competitive advantage. Global communities are asking for greater commitment from companies for ESG before they invest in them. This is great news for women.

Digital technology is another factor that is creating a perfect opportunity for companies to take up more women in STEM. We witnessed how digital technology provided benefits and transformations throughout the COVID crisis. COVID-19's impact has highlighted the benefits of various technologies, such as automation, AI and blockchain. Some mining companies are embracing digital and data optimisation opportunities, to create positive and enduring changes to the workplace for women.

Companies that have invested in improving their digital strategies will have a competitive advantage in the long term. The mining industry will not require strong able-bodied men as before, but increasingly, robots, as AI takes over. A digital economy means the mining industry has to think differently. It's not man versus woman. It is human versus AI robots. It is space vs earth mining. If the mining industry remains male-focussed, it will miss out on recruiting some of the best and brightest who don't look like them, speak like them, or laugh at the same jokes as them.

The only challenge we may face in the implementation of technology is the exclusion of diverse groups in prototypes. Research undertaken by Buolamwini and Gebru (2018), founder of the Algorithmic Justice League, has shown that automated systems used to inform decisions about sentencing produce results that are biased against black people, and that those used for selecting the targets of online advertising can discriminate based on race and gender. When it comes to algorithmic bias in facial analysis, technology and software appeared to work well for white men but less so for everyone else. The implications of Buolamwini's (2018) study provide important insights into diversity and inclusion.

In addition, decarbonisation has become a competitive advantage for early adopters. My view is that mining companies need to consider having separate departments specifically for entrepreneurs to work collaboratively with government and other research institutes to drive innovation. This will help establish new structures to drive the ESG agenda. Roles such as Chief of Diversity and Inclusion, Chief Innovation Officer, and Chief Sustainability Officer are already popular.

The other area that is neglected in ESG reporting is sustainable supply chain sourcing. How much supply spend goes to female-owned companies? Big companies are spending, on average, more than three to five billion dollars on procurement and supply. There is a role here that women can and want to play. Many entrepreneurs, including women, have said they have contacted mining companies with solutions including digital technology and mine community relations but the mining companies want to do business with those who look like them.

True commitment to empowerment will come if mining companies disclose in their sustainability reports who the top ten spends are in their companies, and how much they are spending in the procurement. I wouldn't be surprised if the top 10 suppliers' spend is comprised of less than 5% female-owned companies. This is an opportunity to economically empower women.

We need to use our voices to ensure sustainable change for the mines of the future.

Diversity and inclusion have become business imperatives. The mining industry is about to transform from a boys' club to having more male champions for diversity and inclusion. It is a perfect storm for women in STEM to lean in.

Summary

Are you a woman in STEM or a C-Suite leader in mining who would like access to an executive summary of the survey we did on what it takes to succeed in a male-dominated workplace like mining? Download a free copy of the Executive Summary with profound insights at www.unleashingmysuperpowers.com/bonuses.

CHAPTER 9

BECOMING A GLOBAL THOUGHT LEADER

There is always light. If only we're brave enough to see it.
If only we're brave enough to be it.
– Amanda Gorman

Unleashing Your Superpowers, by Dr. Patience Mpofu

It's your high level of consciousness that says in the midst of adversity,
who stands with you?
You have support, because you are a spiritual being of light
It is that inner power that transcends the normal understanding
of the mind
It is that inner still voice that whispers, 'you are enough'
It is the guiding light that says
You are love, you are compassionate, you are a gift to the world
You know your values and what drives you
It's your Why!
It's an energy that keeps you going.
Whatever you do, it's coming from a place of love
It's beyond self, its understanding that you are because of others
A superpower that propels you to be unstoppable

It's beyond the physical realm.
It is that part of who you want to be remembered for
That inner voice that gives you purpose, meaning, passion
That says 'unleash your superpowers'
That says, 'honour someone's dream'
You know you can lead with purpose
You know you have a gift to share
You know are adding value in this world
You know you have abundance to share
You know you are enough
You are now unstoppable
You are just, enough

'Oh Auntie, that was so amazing. I think I want to be like you when I grow up. I want to do STEM subjects and have a chemical engineering degree,' my niece, Thembelihle, exclaimed.

I often think about that wonderful family holiday in Lesotho, when I told my story and my family encouraged me to write a book to inspire others. I asked myself how I would write such a book for maximum impact when, one day, an idea came like a flash of lightning: the International Women's Forum Fellows Program. When you have a growth mindset as a leader, you are constantly looking for ways to develop yourself.

The IWF began when Elinor Guggenheimer, chair of the New York City Planning Commission, went to a meeting in Philadelphia. When she arrived, she was told that the only women allowed in the building were waitresses and maids. Determined to participate, Elly found a maid's uniform, put it on, and took her rightful place at the table. At that moment, she knew something had to change. In 1974, Elly established the organisation that become IWF.

The program has a legacy component to it, and I knew that would be perfect for me, and I could do some writing while on sabbatical. I quickly grabbed my laptop and checked the deadline for application.

It was in less than a week. I thought I wouldn't make it. That night, I started looking at the requirements. I had previously met the executive director for the Fellows Program at the IWF Conference in Johannesburg in 2014. The next day, I started working on my application.

My former boss and I were discussing my plans. She asked if I wanted to put my name in for the roles that may come up as the company created new structures. It was a bit too late, and I felt as though I would be betraying myself by making that choice. She then asked what my next step would be, apart from spending time with my mum. I told her about the IWF Fellows Program and asked if she could support my application. She was happy to provide a recommendation. I submitted my full application a day before the final deadline, including the rigorous essays that I had spent sleepless nights writing.

* * *

'Patience, take a rest and relax. Do something that you have never done before while on sabbatical. I know one guy who went and did acting lessons and he really enjoyed himself'. This was my former boss Mike's speech on the day of my farewell, in July 2018. We had worked together for more than a year before I started reporting to the head office in Perth. He threw a little farewell dinner for me before I left the organisation. 'I would like to thank you for your contribution, and to be honest, your role was one of the toughest in the region as it had many challenges when you took over. I greatly appreciate the work you did with your team, and here is your gift from us.' I was touched and greatly appreciated the gesture, and my colleagues who came to say goodbye. It is these moments that we treasure, when someone notices and appreciates us. I had completed my last event on my last day at an awards ceremony, to ensure I left all work completed. I was reminded of that proverb about not burning bridges. I always leave my employers on a high note.

The following months after my departure from the corporate world were filled with inner work including meditation and reflection, as well as some physical work that I had neglected for too long: hiking, going to the gym, and swimming. Connecting and spending time with my family, especially my mum, was the best. This period was so precious to me as I realised how much I had sacrificed my well-being for my career.

Sometimes you feel your energy is not in the right place. When a client that I was coaching asked me, 'When do you know it's time to leave?' I told her it was when you get to a certain stage of your career and you realise you want to live your true values. You will want to take advantage of your talents, surrounding yourself with those who support you, in a place where your contributions are recognised.

I had neglected my health and gained so much weight. I didn't have much energy. I needed to prioritise my health. I believed in the saying, 'your health is your new wealth'. I did not want to be a statistic of depression and end up committing suicide. I thought I had fatigue until I read an article by Lapin (2020) on fatigue versus depletion, published during the COVID-19 pandemic. I was depleted, and depletion can lead to depression.

My mother suffered from depression for a long time, and I regularly reflect on how managing your mental state and walking away from situations that can harm you is important. Lapin (2020) says there are two different states of being: fatigue and depletion. The author argues that fatigue is when a muscle or the mind has been used almost to the point of failure, and it requires rest to recuperate. Contrastingly, depletion is when our inner resources of energy have been drained, and this may have no connection to exertion. It means that one can be depleted without feeling tired, and one can be tired without feeling depleted. The key takeaway from the article is that when we are depleted, we need restoration rather than rest or relaxation. Leaders suffer more from depletion than from fatigue, but few recognise this, the author says. This was an *aha* moment for me. I was indeed depleted when I went through restructuring at work. I was busy supporting my team and completely neglected myself.

What followed was what I would call divine intervention. On 1st of August, 2018, exactly a month after I left my corporate job, I received an unexpected email that read: *'Dear Patience, it is my pleasure to inform you that the IWF Leadership Foundation has selected you to participate in the 2018–2019 Fellows Program. Congratulations! You were selected for the Fellows Program from a highly competitive pool of diverse candidates. Comprised of 36 outstanding leaders, the 2018–2019 Fellows Class spans industries, sectors and geographies, with participants from 12 nations: Australia, Bermuda, Canada, China, Indonesia, Jamaica, Mexico, New Zealand, South Africa, Turkey, the United Kingdom and the United States.'*

When I received this news, I was with my sister, Diana, having just completed a great workout with one of the best kick-boxing instructors at Virgin Active in Bryanston. I was ecstatic, to say the least. I was finally going to further develop myself and meet likeminded, accomplished women across the globe while I was on sabbatical, but most important was the Legacy Project, which would motivate me to write this book.

The year-long fellowship included several components: an orientation and training as the cohort's first meeting, followed by participation in the 2018 IWF World Leadership Conference and Gala, which took place from October 21–27 in Miami, Florida. Then in February 2019, we met again in Boston, at Harvard Business School, and lastly in July 2019, at Insead in Paris.

Before the exciting IWF program started, I was busy preparing for my trip to the first item on my bucket list, which was Tony Robbins' Unleashing Your Power Within event, in Sydney in September 2018. It was transformational. I was stunned at the approximately 9000 energy-filled people attending. I can attest to the fact that when you leave the five-day event, you are transformed, as I was. I wanted more. Many things finally made sense, especially when it came to leading oneself. I had been on a roller coaster for many months without taking a break. Tony challenges you with your limiting beliefs. This was big for me. 'What story have you been telling yourself? Change your story.'

At one point in my career, I felt something was preventing me from moving forward and from leading the life I was supposed to be living.

You are the author of your own story. Tony makes you shift your perspective at a deeper level—from feeling helpless, hopeless and blaming, to taking control of your life by turning pain into growth and success. What is the lesson in all of this? You cannot change other people; you can only change yourself. You are responsible for your own success. This was a new chapter for me, and yet another *aha* moment.

I have always been good at taking full ownership and reframing challenges. It took a lot of courage for me to say no and to refuse to be a victim. It may have been at the expense of my financial well-being at that time, but at least I could walk with my head up, knowing I had unleashed my superpowers. How often do we settle for less and then resent people or organisations, when we have the choice to say no?

Knowing your values is important as they define your life choices. We make decisions based on how strong our value systems are versus our opportunities. This is true even with relationships with our spouses or our leaders. This is why it's important for leaders to live the values they have communicated to their employees. I know some of my top values are recognition, integrity, trust, impact, authenticity, respect, love and connection, care and accountability. I walked away from many opportunities in my career because my values were violated, either consciously or unconsciously.

How we do anything is how we do everything. Holding each other accountable for our behaviours by giving and receiving feedback is one way to ensure that we walk the talk of how we want to be perceived by our teams. Feedback is an important part of identifying the behaviours that are derailers as a leader. And as a leader, you feel a certain sense of responsibility as it's not just about you but your teams and the overall organisation as well. So, you outgrow selfishness and consider how to ensure that your team unleashes their superpowers to thrive and create value for the company.

This event with Tony Robbins was just the tip of the iceberg in learning how one's mind can be stretched to build resilience. I became the master of my own destiny at a level that I had never experienced. I had read about mind power and known about affirmations, visualisations, and the like, but I was hungry for more knowledge. My mind, body and soul needed detoxification and renewal. The brain is like a sponge, absorbing from childhood to adulthood. I signed up for further programs that would focus on developing my mind, body, spirit and relationships. The sabbatical had started on a high note and didn't disappoint.

* * *

'What are you doing to honour someone's dream?' This was a challenge that we were given as we thought about our legacy projects at our first cohort for the IWF Fellows Program in Miami, USA, in October 2018. I think about this regularly to ensure that I live a meaningful life. I arrived three days before the program started and took some time to visit a few art galleries and enjoy the beach. This was my second time in Miami, and I was amazed again at the relaxed atmosphere.

On the morning of the first session we all gathered in one of the conference rooms. *Fortune favours the bold and the prepared!* I was feeling unusually nervous. These were all accomplished C-Suite women from all over the world, with 12 nationalities represented. 'Hi, my name is Patience. When my parents gave me this name, I had no clue how much it would test my ability to be patient throughout my life, especially in a male-dominated work environment.' I began telling my story.

The power of storytelling is phenomenal. I love telling and hearing stories. Stories connect people at a different level. When I finished, everyone clapped. Others' stories followed and then we had a break. That was the moment we connected, and it was for life. We laughed, cried, played, and supported each other as sisters. The power of having a community of like-minded women is critical as you expand your social capital.

The rest of the day was filled with transformational learning and growth. We learned how to figure out what our mission is, align it with our values, and use our voice as a force for good. I was interested in meeting Cady Coleman, who had spent 180 days in space. I knew in my heart that I wanted to interview her someday. That day it became a reality.

The most important part of the program and what had initially attracted me was introduced to us—the Legacy Project. Three global leaders from Australia, France and the USA, all IWF Fellows alumni, spoke to us about their legacy projects and gave advice on how to choose the right project. The Legacy Project is about applying the skills we learned in a socially relevant way. Essentially, it's about what mark you will leave behind. What do you want to be remembered for? The question was, *What problem do I want to address in my community or organisation?*

The program was spread over eight months and we were assigned mentors. I had an excellent experience and the sisterhood is still thriving. When it came to selecting my legacy project, I knew I wanted to transform the lives of women in mining. My initial idea was to connect female entrepreneurs in mining with established companies looking to do business in South Africa, but this changed after experiencing some challenges, like getting buy-in from mining companies. I changed the scope towards the end of the year after we finished the program.

I haven't given up and hopefully will be able to impact more women with my soon-to-launch academy. I selected a project that speaks to me, was easier to execute without sponsors, and has supporters globally. I learned important lessons trying to get the project off the ground. Firstly, to know who in your network are supporters. Secondly, to select a project that you and your supporters are passionate about.

Sometimes, as women, we may feel our talents are not recognised, but that could be because we are in the wrong organisations. As a woman leader in the mining industry, I have made decisions that have made me who I am today. As a global leadership coach, my vision is to see more girls and women dare to pursue and advance their careers in STEM and the mining industry. I have faced challenges in my leadership journey that have made me stronger, and I have used the lessons learned to keep moving up in the corporate world. I have made mistakes in my leadership journey that I can share with other women to show them what not to do. I have asked myself what I would tell my younger self if I were to do this all over again.

This speaks to women who are in STEM and the mining industry who feel stuck and don't know if they have made the right choices. Choices determine our destinies. That might be an old cliché, but it's so true. The choices I have made in my leadership journey have led to my success. I want more women who have broken through the glass ceiling to share their stories with other women who are struggling, especially in STEM.

Empowering women in the economy and closing gender gaps in the world of work arc crucial to achieving the 2030 Agenda for Sustainable Development Goals, particularly Goal 5, to achieve gender equality. As I was about to start the project, the COVID-19 pandemic surfaced and shattered all my plans. I was in limbo as I needed to pivot my business and also help other women during what was perhaps the most traumatic time of our lives. I felt there was a sense of urgency for a campaign to help more women succeed in STEM-related professions.

Ask any woman in the STEM field and she'll tell you that the glass ceiling blocking them from C-level positions is real. Despite some progress after centuries of women not being allowed to work, much still needs to be done. It takes more than being a technical specialist in your STEM field to shatter the glass. You need to be a solid performer and consistently deliver as a specialist in your field first, and then have strong leadership capabilities to rise to C-Suite, which often requires a different set of competencies. Closing the gender gap is in the best interests of the mining industry. With the fourth industrial revolution, almost all the jobs of the future will include STEM.

Therefore, I undertook a study over a year to highlight the major barriers that are sustaining gender inequality in STEM-related industries. This provided insights into key success factors in navigating male-dominated workplaces, and helping more women break the barriers holding them back from reaching C-Suite positions.

I organised the study into three phases:

Phase 1: Conducting 30 interviews with women in C-Suite across the globe, and created a 100-day campaign of inspirational stories from these accomplished women leaders who have succeeded in their careers in male-dominated workplaces. Then I did a survey on the major barriers to success in male-dominated workplaces, with 100 women in STEM, with Part A being women in C-Suite, and Part B being middle to senior management. Sixty-five per cent of these women were from the mining industry.

Phase 2: Publishing my book on how I succeeded in a male-dominated work environment as a woman in STEM.

Phase 3: Launching the Unleashing My Superpowers Executive Leadership Academy.

I completed the 100-day campaign and the survey (Phase 1). Some of the important questions were:

- What is the biggest challenge in navigating the male-dominated work environment, from the survey results?
- What are the top 10 barriers to career advancement for women in STEM in Group B vs Group A? How do they differ per industry, per level (specialists to senior vs C-Suite)?
- Does having a role model, coach, mentor or sponsor help to succeed in a workplace? Compare the C-Suite vs specialist to senior manager. What are the differences as a percent?
- What are the top 10 emerging themes of major turning points in the C-Suite leadership journey (epiphany moments) that helped them break through the glass ceiling in their STEM profession?
- What are the top 10 emerging leadership themes that other women can learn from the C-Suite to succeed in a male-dominated work environment that you would like to share?

Below is a snapshot of a summary/comments from the survey results:

- The results show that to move to C-Suite, one needs to have a mentor, a sponsor, a coach and network of like-minded business people.
- The culture in male-dominated workplaces has a major impact on achieving gender diversity.
- More than 90% of women below C-Suite agree with the statement that when women support each other, more women will be successful. We need to leverage the collective power of women. Each woman for herself is a losing strategy.
- Being an advocate, you need to be passionate and have a position, and welcome solutions that advance your cause.
- The worst thing is having women gloss over the real challenges facing many women because they are benefitting from the status quo. Women need to support each other.

The top eight barriers to women's advancement were identified as follows, in order of importance:

- Not having enough women in leadership positions
- Unconscious bias
- Bullying
- Exclusion
- Lack of support
- Male-dominated culture
- Gender discrimination
- Hard work not being recognised

Not Having Enough Women in Leadership Positions

Ninety-eight percent of the women we surveyed said that if there were more women in leadership positions, more women would succeed. In addition, 70% believed the biggest barrier to getting more women promoted is that there are no women in senior positions. Published data does not lie. All one needs to do is to look at the number of women in C-Suite, board or even vice president level to see how committed these mining companies are to closing the gender gap.

Unconscious Bias

Lean in on the table, but when the table is taken away and the door is shut in your face, leaning in doesn't help. We talked about leaning in, but this assumes that you have resources to lean on and the knowledge of where to lean in. I recall one time when I was having a casual conversation with a colleague, and she mentioned something about how another colleague drank almost half of this amazing vintage wine that she had. She asked, 'Don't you remember that day?' I couldn't remember the occasion and asked when that was. She said, 'Last month'. I presumed I had not been invited. Some of these informal meetings happen and you are not aware of them. How do we level the playing field if you are the only person who looks like you and you are not invited to sit at the table?

So many stereotypes are barriers to women's advancement to move into positions traditionally held by men. Stereotyping can also play a role in shaping the feedback women receive. It's been shown that people hire based on who they feel comfortable with. White males are more comfortable talking to people who look like them. This brings us to the concept of unconscious bias. As a young girl, like many others, I often questioned whether I was good enough. I always found myself being drawn to science, and excelling, despite challenges. I have experienced many examples of unconscious bias as a young, educated black woman. A few examples include being questioned about whether a credit card was mine and needing my husband's authorisation to use it, as it had Dr. P Mpofu on it. When I travelled with my male partner he was recorded as Dr. P Mpofu, and I was recorded as Mrs. Mpofu.

Exclusion

We need to confront the elephant in the room, the untransformed part of society, with frank and open conversations. We cannot deny that some racist and sexist behaviour exists. The other dimension is ageism. I recall one day when a lady was appointed to a leadership team I worked for. The first thing she said when she saw me was, 'I didn't know that the mining industry employs very young people in Exco.' I was violating the stereotypical expectations of a black woman. I am someone who also speaks my mind, and this will inevitably offend some. Someone once said women should stop being politely angry.

In my view, being your authentic self means really feeling emotions. Yes, women may be labelled emotional, but we *are* different. I have shown my emotions once, when Marikana happened. COVID-19 has shown us that it's okay to be vulnerable as a leader; otherwise, you are totally disconnected from your teams. What matters is how quickly we move on from being emotional. We want to be strong and ignore others' unkind statements and actions, but sometimes that means bottling up negative emotions, which is not healthy. Even as an entrepreneur, running my own company, I face many challenges with some males.

The one that stands out in my mind was when one male, who runs a mining magazine, asked to feature me as a successful CEO and owner of a mining company in his magazine, which was still relatively new to the market. After I sent him my profile, he portrayed me on his website as someone who worked for him as a contributor, completely misrepresenting me. When I confronted him, he wasn't even apologetic, and was continuing to use my name for his company's benefit. The sad part is that he is a fellow black man. It was so disappointing.

Bullying

Bullying was highlighted as one of the invisible barriers in male-dominated workplaces. Bullies, if unchecked, can do considerable harm to staff morale, productivity and teamwork (Manuela 2020). Some traits associated with a toxic leader are: lack of remorse, lack of empathy, and not accepting responsibility. Many toxic leaders are master manipulators who will use every trick in the book to achieve their goals (McClean et al 2021). There are those who are your competitors and those who will bring you down.

Bullies are unable to experience deep human emotions, especially love and compassion. Take Thomas as an example. He appeared to have all the leadership qualities required for the role he was in. Being a high performer, he came across as charming and intelligent, but he was emotionally abusive, vindictive, and sometimes aggressive, undermining anyone who disagreed with him. People wonder why leadership praised and promoted his behaviour, when he was detrimental to the culture of the organisation. No amount of grit and determination can make teams pull through in such a culture.

There is a saying: *power corrupts*. Power sometimes does not reside with the leader but the master manipulator. Most of the time, it's the informal power that can corrupt. Toxic leaders use these informal powerful people for their personal objectives. An example is a leader who allows a subordinate to share negative views of co-workers, wasting valuable time under the guise of *networking* or *building relationships*. This creates negative energy that alienates others.

Gossip also diminishes the leader, since accepting the flaws of others is the first step towards figuring out how to deal with them effectively, which is precisely what good leaders do. As a leader, it's important to understand that politics exists whether we like it or not. In my sessions I coach people on how to identify and deal with toxic people in the workplace.

I was talking to a lady at a networking function when she mentioned that her company had a Thomas. Everyone knew that some of his behaviours were unacceptable, but no one dared to raise the issue. To make matters worse, he was one of the top leaders. When she joined the organisation, she asked another female employee about him and she laughed off the question with, 'Oh, Tommy, he's good. You'll get used to him. He's a great guy. It's just that sometimes he can be very abrasive, but he is a great leader, and you know, he has talent.' Talent? A great leader? According to whose standards? There is a difference between confidence and ego. He would bully and ridicule people in meetings. She didn't recall ever having a productive meeting when Tommy was present.

One time when she was supposed to chair an important meeting, he said that she should not be in the meeting as she was not needed. Many organisations tolerate such behaviour. This speaks to the culture of bullying and intimidation. At performance time, she was rated low in comparison with the rest of the team. Tommy, on the other hand, who was perceived as *talented* although he showed no credible results, was always rated high. It was a blow to her career, so she ended up leaving the organisation.

Some of the behaviours that are detrimental to women's career advancement to C-Suite positions include deliberate undermining. Such behaviour will inevitably lead to a woman leader having negative emotions. We are energetic beings with empathy. Energy is everything. An inclusive work environment will encourage everyone to contribute. Creating positive energy makes employees feel valued and excited about their work.

Toxic workplaces make people negative and unproductive, which ultimately impacts organisational performance. In such situations, shareholders need not look far to understand why the organisation has underperformed versus its peers. Toxic leadership can result in low morale, leading to low productivity, leading to low shareholder returns. One mistake leaders make is developing their subordinates with executive leadership development programs, but failing to develop themselves when it comes to leadership. Culture eats profits—period.

Lack of Support

Despite the obvious benefits of rising through the ranks, it comes with immense pressure, scrutiny and time commitments. Further, the lack of work-life balance can take a toll on physical and mental health, as well as relationships. This has been highlighted as one of the barriers to women's advancement in male-dominated workplaces. With remote working due to COVID-19, how can organisations support women to integrate life and work?

Male-Dominated Culture

King (2020), in her book *The Fix,* says the idea of *fixing* women is a problem as the work environment was and still is designed for males. The author says imploring women to adopt behaviours that characterise successful men creates a culture that paints women as deficient and devalues diverse working styles. The focus on *fixing* women steers resources away from anti-discrimination initiatives that could actually make a difference.

Culturally, men are associated with leadership qualities and women with nurturing qualities, which makes it difficult for women in mining to be taken seriously. Many still believe that nurturing should be women's first role in society. This is especially prevalent in some developing countries where economic empowerment resides with men. Certain work environments were also structured for males only, particularly the mining industry. In Chapter 8, I discussed how mining companies can re-design the mines of the future to be more inclusive. You will read in Chapter 10 some suggestions for what leaders in these male-dominated workplaces can do.

Summary

Some of the barriers highlighted by women remind me of this dilemma: *Be nice but not too nice. Be assertive but not aggressive. Be confident but have humility. Be successful but modest with it. Be kind but not walked over. Have EQ but don't be emotional.*

From Not Good Enough to Most Influential in Mining in Africa

I cried so hard that I couldn't control myself. I couldn't believe this was happening. *Is it true?* I asked myself. *This is it?* I was in complete shock. Everyone came when they heard my sobs. 'What's wrong? Are you okay?' they kept asking. I was just too emotional; it was too much. My voice disappeared. I couldn't speak. In some ways, the universe will always say *yes* to your thoughts. If your thoughts are positive and full of love and gratitude, then reality will bend towards the positive. If your thoughts are negative, then reality will contort in such a way that it produces negative results. Recognising these rules of nature will help you steer your own experiences in the right direction and help produce the results you want.

There are so many women who have done so much. This can't be. My sister Diana and my son William kept saying I should stop it. When I arrived at the venue at the Hilton Hotel in Johannesburg, South Africa, I was told I had won two awards: Most Influential Woman in Government and Industry in the mining industry sector for South Africa and the southern African region, by CEO Global. This is one of the most respected integrated media companies, founded in June 2001, which has gone from strength to strength on the African continent. CEO is the publisher of the monthly business title *CEO Magazine*, as well as three special editions: *Africa's Most Influential Women in Business and Government, Women in Motion* and *TITANS–Building Nations*.

Yes, I am enough, and I deserved the title. The award represents something deep for me: it is a symbol for the struggle of a black woman in mining. I embrace it on behalf of all women. The fight for gender equality is a moral and economic issue. Women make not just good leaders, but great ones.

Do not fret or have any anxiety about anything, but in every circumstance and in everything, by prayer and petition, with thanksgiving, continue to make your wants known to God.

I always randomly pick a scripture from the Bible before going to bed and, this day, I picked a scripture about gratitude. I read it before dozing off, and I indeed had a feeling of gratitude. My cup overflows.

Receiving Most Influential Woman in Mining award

Exercise

To help you get to know yourself better and figure out what gives you meaning, I have created a template taken from the book *IKIGAI: The Japanese Secret to a Long and Happy Life* by Garcia and Miralles (2017). Go to www.unleashingmysuperpowers.com/bonuses.

CHAPTER 10

UNLEASHING OUR SUPERPPOWERS

Unleashing my superpowers is finding and using my voice to be a catalyst for change. It is to say, I am enough, I lead with purpose, share my gifts with the world and honour someone's dreams so that they too can unleash their superpowers.
—Dr. Patience Mpofu

Our Deepest Fear, by Marianne Williamson

Our deepest fear is not that we are inadequate.
Our deepest fear is that we are powerful beyond measure.
It is our light, not our darkness
That most frightens us.

We ask ourselves
Who am I to be brilliant, gorgeous, talented, fabulous?
Actually, who are you not to be?
You are a child of God.

Your playing small
Does not serve the world.
There's nothing enlightened about shrinking
So that other people won't feel insecure around you.

We are all meant to shine,
As children do.
We were born to make manifest
The glory of God that is within us.

It's not just in some of us;
It's in everyone.

And as we let our light shine,
We unconsciously give other people permission to do the same.
As we're liberated from our own fear,
Our presence automatically liberates others.

Unleashing My Superpowers:
Being Compassionate About Self: The Wounded Elephant

I have come close to death four times. The first was when I almost drowned as a young girl, as narrated in Chapter 2. The second and third times were when I had an altitude reaction in Chile and a similar incident in Lesotho. The fourth was when I was sure a huge elephant was going to attack us at a safari in South Africa.

As I have mentioned, I am an outdoor lover and I enjoy African safaris. I have since trained as a wildlife photographer and on one memorable occasion, I trained at a great safari in South Africa. It was a four-hour drive from Johannesburg, and we arrived just before midday. The theory part of the workshop started at midday and was followed by the practical part, a game drive where we could practise all the skills we had learned. Our game ranger warned us there was a huge elephant that had survived being poached but unfortunately, she had not only lost part of her left tusk, but also some of her cubs. You can imagine how she must have felt.

Poaching is an enormous problem in these areas, particularly rhino and elephant poaching. The poaching crisis began in 2008, with increasing numbers of rhinos and elephants killed for their horns and tusks. Elephants are mainly poached for their ivory tusks which are used for ornaments, jewellery, billiard balls, piano keys and other items that humans enjoy. South Africa holds the majority of the world's rhinos and elephants and thus has been hit hardest by criminal poachers. Poaching has decreased across the continent but there are still reports of rhinos being killed every day and there is a lot more to be done, as reported by the Save the Rhino Organisation.

Our party of eight climbed aboard the safari car for the game drive. As usual, we saw impalas and springboks but surprisingly, we hadn't seen elephants. After about an hour of driving and great photography opportunities, the game ranger spotted the huge elephant he had mentioned earlier. We started taking pictures while she was pretty far away, but two ladies sitting behind us couldn't see properly, so they asked the ranger to move a bit closer. Just as he did, the elephant started charging toward our car, flapping her ears. I have seen many elephants in Botswana but none came close to the size of the one I saw that day.

We pleaded with the ranger to turn and drive away, as we could sense danger. 'It's too late,' he replied. 'If we try to drive away, it will think we have come to hunt it for its tusk and they have long memories… it will still be angry at losing its cubs and tusk. Let's stay calm. No-one should move or take pictures; it will not harm us if we show it love and not fear.'

We were all scared to death as this massive animal angrily flapped her ears. She came right next to the car and was almost double the size of it. The elephant stretched her trunk to the front of the car on the left side where an orthopaedic specialist was sitting next to the driver, and wrapped it around his neck. I was sitting behind him and my thought was that this was not real. The doctor was shaking and drenched in sweat. I thought for a second that the elephant was going to throw him out of the truck, or turn our car upside down and crush it. Then she untangled herself, and what happened next was something I could never have imagined.

The elephant came right next to where I was sitting and performed the same manoeuvre, wrapping her trunk around my neck as if she was going to pull me out of the car. I'm sure my heart stopped beating. Not only was the trunk heavy, but the skin was as rough as stone. It was surreal. Suddenly, I remembered how I had left my will. Oh s…! I still had my ex as the beneficiary and hadn't gotten around to updating it. I realised I hadn't spoken with my son that morning nor my mum and sisters. I wanted to cry, but my partner who was sitting next to me squeezed my hand as if to say, 'You will be okay'.

In situations like these, when you can almost smell death, the mind turns to the supernatural. I took a deep inward breath and said a silent prayer to God to rescue me. I visualised a golden light and God lifting the elephant trunk from my shoulder. I was calm and just surrendered to fate. In what felt like an hour but was actually less than a few minutes, the massive animal let go of me. She repeated this performance with the two people seated behind me, but for some reason retained her hold on the last lady who was sobbing for longer. The ranger calmly said to her, 'Stop showing fear and be calm and it will be okay'. Eventually, the huge elephant released her and slowly walked away without harming anyone. We all breathed a huge sigh of relief, knowing ours was a near death experience.

Elephant at the safari

I have been on more than 15 safari trips, including the great migration at Masai Mara in Kenya, and fortunately, never again did I have such a close encounter with imminent mortality, although I did almost come face to face with a cheetah at Mahali Mzuri in Kenya while having a massage. That was also a scary experience but the difference was that the elephant was angry. She had been carrying her anger for a long time and therefore did not trust anything that looked like her enemy. She was carrying past hurts and a belief system that a safari car meant danger, since she had lost her tusk and dear cubs.

We, too, carry past hurts, scars and traumas that have become our belief system, mostly at a subconscious level. When we experience something resembling the original trauma, it triggers those belief systems and feelings like fear and anger. The question to ask is: what made the elephant decide not to attack us, as surely we resembled the poachers?

This episode demonstrates the power of mindset shift, and of energy and the belief system. Firstly, the game ranger—who was our leader—remained composed. He knew we were facing death, but he was calm, or pretended to be calm. Everything is energy. His calming energy was contagious. He calmly said, 'The elephant is charging fast. It's too late for us to move now and I suggest everyone keep calm and give the elephant vibes of love, and everything will be okay.' His demeanour and energy said *we will be okay*. He only told us afterwards that it was the first time the elephant had come this close and that he had never experienced this situation before. Game rangers know how to avoid getting too close to an angry elephant.

The second component of this episode is the belief system. Despite my prayer to God, at some level, I believed I was going to be okay. The third component is vibes of compassionate love and not fear. When someone is angry at you, what do you do? Is it better to give them love or to retaliate with anger and resentment? Have you heard the saying that angry people need more love? Energy is contagious. Compassionate love is vital. When we face adversity as leaders, we need to practise compassion with self, and with others. This is unleashing your superpowers as a leader.

Facing My Fears and Removing Limiting Belief Systems to Unleash My Superpowers

Most of us recognise that we need to change to move ahead, but that is easier said than done. Our brains love habits, and the mind is a powerful force. I found NLP techniques to be great for removing self-limiting beliefs. The neural system favours the path of least resistance, which is why changing familiar behaviours is uncomfortable.

There is no guarantee that you will not face challenges in life. What matters is how you rise above them. After being made redundant at my previous job in 2018, I hit rock bottom. When you go through a setback in life, such as being overlooked for a promotion, or you suffer retrenchment, it's common to respond in one of two ways: either we become defensive and blame others, or we berate ourselves.

A study by Chen (2018) has found that either response is helpful. What she suggests is very interesting. She says to treat yourself as you would a friend in a similar situation: be kind, understanding, and encouraging. Directing that type of response toward ourselves is known as self-compassion, and it's been the focus of a good deal of research in recent years. Self-compassion, unlike self-esteem, doesn't involve judging the self or others. Instead, it creates a sense of self-worth because it leads you to genuinely care about your own well-being and recovery after a setback. Leaders with high levels of self-compassion demonstrate three behaviours: they are kind rather than judgmental about their own mistakes, they recognise that failure is a shared human experience, and they take a balanced approach to negative emotions when they stumble or fall short, whereby they allow themselves to feel bad, but they don't let negative emotions take over.

Self-compassion does more than help people recover from failure or setbacks; it triggers leaders to adopt a growth mindset. There are benefits to adopting a *growth* rather than a *fixed* approach to performance. Leaders with a fixed mindset see personality traits and abilities, including their own, as set in stone. They believe that who they are today is essentially who they will be in five years from now. In contrast, leaders who have a growth mindset view personality traits and abilities as malleable. They see the potential for growth and thus are more likely to try to improve, to put in effort, to practice, and to stay positive and optimistic. Research suggests that self-compassion triggers leaders to adopt a growth mindset. A sign that a leader has a growth mindset is his or her willingness to keep trying to do better after receiving negative feedback.

After leaving my corporate job, I went on what I would call a self-discovery and personal development journey. I applied for the IWF Fellows Program and solicited for an Insead 360-degree assessment from my ex-colleagues, the team I had led, and my former boss. I am constantly trying to improve myself as a leader as that is something I have control over. In addition to that, I wanted to challenge myself and my belief systems, to push myself out of my comfort zone. I therefore invested in a Tony Robbins program held in Fiji in November 2019.

Fiji is one of the most beautiful places I have ever been to, not just because of the amazing beaches and landscape, but also because the people were as friendly as South Africans. There was something magical about that place. Every woman should consider a visit to Fiji and have a Fijian massage.

Tony Robbins takes you to another level and challenges you. I knew I still had limiting beliefs that were holding me back. *I am not good enough!* This was re-enforced from a young age. We carry those limiting beliefs at a subconscious level. I will tell you my story of how I faced my fears and removed the limiting belief systems hidden in my subconscious mind.

How I Faced My Fears and Removed My Limiting Belief Systems

'I'm stuck, I can't move,' I shouted at the top of my voice. I was feeling scared, alone, and I had no idea what to do. Then I started to reflect: *What was I thinking? What have I done? I am not good enough. This is not for me. I shouldn't have done this.* All these thoughts raced through my mind when on Day 2 of the program in Fiji, we did a transformational exercise outside the beautiful resort where we were staying. The weather was glorious, and there must have been close to a hundred people at the conference.

I was staying at Namale Resort, where I had slept like a baby. I had booked this program almost 18 months in advance, using my redundancy package to fund it, as I knew I needed this as part of my self-discovery journey. I was keen to face my fears and change the belief systems that were holding me back. We were divided into two groups and given the task to climb a pole, small in diameter, but 20 metres long. I had been bungy jumping before, but this seemed too hard. I eventually summoned the courage to climb it, being one of the last ones to do so. Only two people could climb at a time. I climbed with so much cheering from all my group members. *That wasn't so bad after all,* I thought, as I approached the top.

Dr. Patience Mpofu at the top of the pole in Fiji in November 2019

The idea was to climb to the top in a harness, and then, when you got up there, to balance your feet on the top section and stand upright. The intended outcome was to break through our fears and self-limiting beliefs. The biggest challenge was the surface area of the pole, which was almost the size of a dinner plate. As you reached the top, you had to try to maintain balance to get your whole body up, and due to the size of the pole, this was almost impossible for me. I eventually managed to dislodge myself and lift my whole body to get to the top.

The next challenge was trying to balance and stand on the pole, made difficult by the length of the pole and the slight breeze. I was stuck. Initially, everyone was clapping and encouraging me, but later, after I had been stuck for 20 minutes or so, people got tired and stopped clapping. I was alone. I was terrified. I considered myself an idiot for tackling a challenge meant for more clever people. I felt oddly that I had let everyone down. *I am not meant for this!* I thought to myself.

There were a few people who didn't give up, including the coach, Dan, and a friend, Hayley, who I met there and later became friends with in Sydney. They kept encouraging me, but I was not listening. Eventually, Dan said, 'Patience, take a deep breath and listen carefully to me. We all love you here, don't we team A?'

They all erupted, 'Yes! Peak Performance with Patience, Peak Performance with Patience… You can do this… You got this Patience.' Instantly, my energy shifted. I was calmer and not fearful anymore. I felt encouraged and part of a team. I was not alone in this struggle. I had one hundred people supporting me. In fact, the other group from the other team also started joining in, encouraging me. Dan then said, 'Listen to me now, to what you need to do, and listen very carefully. Lift your hand, and place both hands on the pole that's hanging in front of you, then lift one leg and place your foot on the pole while balancing your hands so that you don't freefall. Then, once one foot is on the pole, you will be able to lift your whole body and the second foot. Just keep holding the rope with your hands.'

As I became calmer, I realised I was holding the rope with one hand. The moment I grabbed it with the second hand and lifted my bum off the pole, I felt lighter and I could balance myself. I did what I was told, and *boom!* I stood up, with my hands wide open, letting go of the rope, to huge applause erupting from the crowd. They were all cheering for me. I was ecstatic. I learned that day that making sound decisions will not happen when you are stressed or fearful.

'Yes, I am a Peak Performer! Yes, I am enough! Yes, I got this! Yes, I unleashed my superpowers!' I shouted with joy. I tried to grab the trapeze that was dangling nearby, and didn't manage to, but that was normal as only one or two people managed to grab it, and that was the final challenge. I was so happy and felt a huge sense of accomplishment.

How many people feel stuck in careers, or after being retrenched or passed over for promotion? You start with shock and denial and move on to anger at whoever you deem was responsible, be it a company or a person. I certainly went through this grieving process. We all go through adversity in our lives and careers and the leaders who rebound from such failures instead of getting stuck in grief or blame will actively explore how they contributed to what went wrong, and evaluate what they would do differently if given a chance. They also gather feedback from a variety of people. I already had feedback.

You see, I had a story playing in my head. I had a self-limiting belief that I could not stand on that pole in Fiji. I spent almost twenty minutes on something that could have taken less than five minutes. I became fearful, and yet when I was climbing at the beginning, I was courageous and competent. Then I got stuck. Fear drives people to adopt poor judgment. Fear is 'False Evidence Appearing Real'! As the late Nelson Mandela once said, 'I learned that courage was not the absence of fear, but the triumph over it. The brave man is not he who does not feel afraid, but he who conquers that fear.'

Challenge your assumptions. Ask yourself: *Is it true?* What we focus on is what we can control. I was doubting myself, feeling like an imposter, a fraud. But once I changed my self-limiting belief system and my story, I stepped up and faced my fears and unleashed my superpowers to succeed. Believing in myself was necessary, and most importantly, I had a coach who never gave up on me. As leaders, how many of us are like coach Dan or Hayley?

Sometimes our teams need a cheerleader to help them through challenges or provide guidance to unleash their superpowers. Who are you cheering for as a leader in mining to help women navigate their careers and unleash their superpowers? What should leaders be doing to help women succeed in a male-dominated workplace? After this phenomenal event in Fiji, I now had the courage to pursue my Legacy Project with confidence. I approached all the women in my network and I was humbled by the positive response from the women I invited to join the campaign.

The Legacy Project: Phase 1: 100 Day Campaign of Inspirational Women

As part my Legacy Project—as explained in Chapter 9—I conducted 30 interviews with women from across the globe, to explore exactly what it takes to succeed in a male-dominated workplace. The women are mostly C-Suite and board level and are from various different industries. I also interviewed global women who are well known for leadership. Not only did it provide me with insight into my own leadership journey, but it also added to my body of knowledge on what it takes for women to succeed in male-dominated work environments. I wanted to hear different perspectives, and to share with women who are trying to break through the glass ceiling, especially in the mining industry and STEM professions.

Below is a summary of Peak Performance strategies to achieve that I classified under my leadership framework:

Leading Self

- Know yourself, your values, your mission, what makes you happy, your anchor, your own belief system: What is the story you keep telling yourself?

- Have confidence, not arrogance, and the courage to ask for what you want and deserve.
- Practice continuous self-development and know when to leave. This was echoed by many women leaders. Sometimes we overstay where we are not wanted.
- Embrace coaching and mentorship. Having a network of people inside and outside the organisation to help you navigate your career progression is super important.
- Leverage other peoples' wisdom.
- Have self-care and compassion for yourself.
- Know that you are enough.
- Relish your supportive family and friends.

Leading Others

- Work where you are supported.
- Speak about your achievements.
- Develop relationships with your subordinates, peers and leaders.
- Networking is important, both internally and externally.

Leading Business

- We need visionary leaders who value diversity.
- We need more male champions to advocate for women.
- We need more female role models.
- We need an inclusive and supportive environment with spiritual and cultural intelligence.
- We need a workplace culture that is progressive in supporting gender diversity, equity and inclusion.
- We need a workplace that is designed for everyone.

Closing the gender gap in male-dominated workplaces can only happen if the decision-makers at the highest levels are on board, and it is men who lead these organisations. This is a perfect opportunity to change the narrative for future generations. Seeing more female role models in leadership positions can inspire other women to believe that they too can make it. I often get comments like, 'If you, Dr. Patience Mpofu, our role model for many years, with a PhD in mining and 25 years of experience, ended up leaving the industry, how can we succeed in this industry?' I often say, I still haven't left the industry and that is why I am writing this book—to get more women involved and be the change I want to see. I am very much in the industry and I am now using my story and other women's stories to inspire more women to succeed.

How the Mining Industry Can Unleash its Superpowers to Be a Champion for Women in STEM

The workplace was, and still is, not made for women. This is likely to change for the mines of the future due to various factors like ESG requirements as discussed in Chapter 8. With how much mining companies have invested over the years in recruiting more women with special leadership programs, sponsoring women has become more essential. This brings me back to my argument about why we need more women at the decision-making table, not on the sidelines. To the males, my question is: *What is your legacy? What do you want your granddaughters to remember you for?* If more women unleash their superpowers, our world will expand with opportunities for all.

Transformational change requires transformational leadership, not small-step change, if we are to achieve gender equality by 2030.

There she stood, making history. Everyone was inspired by Amanda Gorman, that young American poet and activist who writes about oppression, racial issues, feminism, marginalisation and the African diaspora. In 2021, she delivered the poem *The Hill We Climb* at the inauguration ceremony of U.S. President Joe Biden and Vice-President Kamala Harris. One of her famous lines that has inspired many: *For while we have our eyes on the future, history has its eyes on us.*

This famous line by Amanda inspires us to reflect on our past and envision the future. We have the power to change the narrative for future generations to come. According to the World Economic Forum's latest Global Gender Gap Report, at the current rate, global gender equality is still 130 years away. The first question we should ask is: *What does the new workplace look like and how can we redesign it to be inclusive and gender equal?* Most of the time, gender biases are subtle and not necessarily intentional or malicious, as explained by most women leaders we interviewed. The problem with these subtle behaviours is that they can lead to systemic unfavourable treatment of individuals based on their gender, denying them equal opportunities. Unless leaders of these male-dominated industries understand and acknowledge how stereotypes and unconscious biases perpetuate the problem, women will continue to be left behind.

Leaders need to look within themselves and not only encourage women to aspire to leadership, but be male advocates for diversity and inclusion. In order to move forward, sometimes leaders need to take bold action. Leaders can support women not to shrink themselves to please, but rather, unleash their superpowers to excel. The workplace was created by men for men. It is time for leaders to reflect on what an inclusive workplace looks like. Business and government working together can create a new economic and social narrative for action and accelerate the process of change.

It is worth asking ourselves this question again: *What does it take for women to get to C-Suite or board positions in a male-dominated workplace?* Below are some suggestions for leaders. This is what I believe will move the needle the most and reduce the 103 years it will take to close the gender gap.

Firstly, leaders of this industry need to get more women in C-Suite and board leadership positions in mining. As reported by S&P Global Market Intelligence (2020), women make up just 14.9% of mining companies' executive ranks, 18.1% of the industry's board positions and 13.2% of the sector's C-suite executive roles. From a survey we conducted across the globe of women in C-Suite in male-dominated workplaces (STEM),

98% of the women said if there were more women in leadership positions, more women would succeed.

70% believe the biggest barrier to getting more women promoted is that there are no women in senior positions.

The second step is the process of recruitment of these C-Suite and board level women leaders as this is where unconscious biases reside. Recruitment should be blind to remove biases. A male leader will sponsor another C-Suite/board level male leader who looks like him, talks like him and laughs at the same jokes as him.

Studies have shown that male leaders are likely to sponsor other male leaders but given a choice between a white woman and black woman, they will choose the white woman (Sandberg, 2013). How can we get more male leaders to sponsor qualified women to C-Suite and board positions? A study by Bohnet (2016) has shown that diversity and inclusion can be achieved if organisations redesign their practises and create new designs that make it easier for our biased minds to adjust to different thinking. A simple first step is to have a no-name, no-gender policy on CVs, including CVs submitted by the executive search firms. Bohnet (2016) calls it a design decision. Bad design, whether consciously or unconsciously chosen, leads to bad outcomes. Bias is built into our practises, not just into our minds.

We need more visibility of women in C-Suite or board positions as role models to inspire younger women and girls. An example is how I was inspired by being led by a female CEO in a mining company. I have decided to make it my mission to showcase every woman leader in C-Suite or board in the mining industry to inspire other women. We have already led a successful campaign for women in STEM and we will now focus specifically on women in mining. In addition, we need to celebrate the male champions who are making this happen.

We need to fast track a pipeline of women in middle to senior positions by supporting them with the services of executive coaches to help them navigate the complex leadership challenges in the work environment. From the same survey, more than 81% of global women in C-Suite we interviewed said having a coach and mentor helped them with navigating the work environment. I am launching an academy to ensure no one is left behind. Investment in such programs can only add value to organisations' bottom line. I recall being approached by a consultant for a mining company to provide executive coaching services for more than 100 women. I thought what a great initiative. Three months down the line, I still haven't received any feedback on the initiative, which is unfortunate as I was ready to help transform the organisation.

Throughout my career, I have been part of a community of likeminded people. This is important for networking. Our survey showed that 84% said having a good network and belonging to a group of likeminded people has helped them break the glass ceiling in their careers. Mining companies should sponsor such organisations to help women.

The C-Suite women or those appointed in board positions will also need to support other women as they rise. Any woman who doesn't support another woman is detrimental to closing the gender gap. Women should hold each other accountable. Of the women we surveyed, 98% believe that when women support each other, more women will succeed.

This is what I call unleashing others' superpowers to help them succeed. Let's all get more women to rise and celebrate their achievements, while also celebrating the male champions who are making this work. We are because of you!

Leading From Your Heart and Mind and Finding Meaning

I was flying from South Africa to Johannesburg, then to Sydney, Australia, and, as usual, I found myself in a bookshop at one of the airports where I found *The Power of Meaning: The true route to happiness* by Emily Esfahani. This book was profound for me. I realised there was a time when I lost my identity temporarily. Most people do. This often occurs when people retire without having planned their next step. It can be a total shock to your system as you lose the status, power, and most importantly, meaning that you had while working. This is especially true for men who have worked their entire lives and have not connected with their families.

They may have burned bridges and created enemies to get to the top, lost loved ones as they rose, or perhaps did not spend much time with their children. Even when they did have family time, they may have had interruptions from phone calls and Zoom meetings, or had to spend weekends on their laptops. In our digital world, most kids are distracted by their devices and do not want to have a conversation with their parents. Then, along came COVID-19, which reset the scene, creating a new norm where families had to be together in one house 24 hours a day. Some marriages fell apart when couples found they were married to a stranger for whom they had lost all passion. Those without families suddenly found themselves alone.

Smith (2017) challenges us to lead a more meaningful life so that when our final moment on earth arrives, we will be at peace. She encourages her readers to create something significant that will make life worthwhile. There is a story in the book of a researcher who did a study on terminally ill patients who wanted a hastened death. He found that they wanted their lives to end not because they were in so much pain but because they had lost meaning in life. This is where the researcher noted the importance of creating meaning.

A legacy is a part of you that will remain even after you are dead. Ensure that there is something you will be remembered for by your family, community, or business. Reflecting on my legacy shifted my perspective and gave me more meaning than I had when I was employed. I became more purposeful about living my values and who I spent time with. My family took on greater significance. I hope this message encourages readers who are leaders in the mining industry to consider their legacy when it comes to inclusivity and not allowing discrimination in their workplaces.

In summary, women are not entitled; they want what is fair and equitable. Assertiveness is not aggression. Asking for what we want is not arrogance. Asking for a seat at the table is not demanding. Calling out bullies is not being difficult. Refusing to be used and abused is not antagonism. It is time for women to stop being politely angry, and to use their voices. Any male leader who is serious about moving toward a more equal world can make this a priority and be part of the solution to closing the gender gap.

The reason I call it unleashing my superpowers is because you need to unleash something extra in order to be the change you want to see in the world. It's about stepping out of your comfort zone and being a catalyst for change. We need institutions and leaders, especially in the mining industry, to leverage their powerful networks to promote more women in leadership positions. Unleash your superpowers as a male leader and use your power, influence and network to effect positive change and help women succeed.

This is the reason why I took sabbatical leave—to be the change I want to see in the world and unleash my superpowers. Taking sabbatical leave allowed me to start the journey of self-discovery and personal development. I attended an impactful program that helped me to heal so that I could become my best self. Taking a sabbatical helped me reset my priorities. Who you spend time with is who you become. If you mix with toxic people, you become toxic. If you spend time with people who possess a growth mindset, that's who you become. I took the time to get to know *me* and found what my passion was, what I am really good at, and what the world needs. By connecting with my true self and inner wisdom, I can now form deeper and more meaningful connections with people. I learned what it takes to build peak performance teams and help leaders tap into their infinite intelligence.

The ability to forgive is not something a lot of people have. I certainly had to learn. For me, grace is about developing a relationship with God and continuously having a dialogue with him through prayer. I usually say to God, *Use me for a purpose greater than me.* It is more about service to others than self. When you learn to forgive, you free yourself to become the best version of yourself. And the person you must learn to forgive the most is yourself.

So, what moved the needle the most in my career? There were many elements. I believe that everything happens for a reason. Obstacles, challenges and disasters are at the root of wisdom.

Everything that happens—good or bad—contains a lesson. Most importantly, you create your own worldview. Being led by a woman in mining reshaped my belief system about what success could look like when we have more female leaders as role models. Living my true values, knowing that I am enough, and leading with authenticity are what moved the needle the most.

Narrating my story to my family inspired my niece to take STEM subjects in high school. I hope that many more girls and women are inspired by this book. I also hope that by the time the reader finishes this story, they will have gained insight into how my story unfolded and that each turn had a lesson that they can take away with them. Today, my life and work are in the service of others. I am constantly asking myself, *How can I help others unleash their superpowers?* Every person has superpowers within them.

As leaders, we have a responsibility to unleash our superpowers and help others do the same. Our energy is contagious. The world needs leaders with a new set of competencies that are more human-centred. If we approach leading others with courage, empathy and confidence, we create an environment that allows those around us to thrive in their creativity. It goes beyond self to a higher level of consciousness that Mandela epitomised. He unleashed his superpower in jail and ultimately became president of his country. The future is bright.

My challenge to you as the reader: Imagine that you are at the end of your life with only days to live. When you reflect on the way you led your life, are you happy with what you see? Did you live a fulfilling life? What would people say about you as a leader? If you could live your life over again, what would you do differently? When you consider your life in retrospect, you will want it to appear beautiful and abundant rather than ugly and desolate.

I have summarised my leadership strategies on what it takes to succeed in a male-dominated mining workplace (STEM) with what I call **The Peak Performance Leadership Model**.

The Peak Performance Leadership Model

Summary

With my coaching and consulting work, I am building a community. We help women use their voices to unleash their superpowers and realise their mission to succeed in male-dominated (STEM) workplaces like mining. I also help organisations unleash their teams' superpowers by creating an inclusive, compassionate, gender-equal environment where everyone feels included and heard, and consequently bring 100% of themselves to work. I have an innate understanding of what it takes to achieve in a male-dominated work environment. My voice was lost at some point in my career but when I found it, I could begin to unleash my superpowers. It feels incredibly refreshing to be my authentic self.

Use your voice for good, and raise it if you have to. If you're still not heard, go outside and use it with greater force. That is truly unleashing your superpowers. I owe everything I am today to the hard times I have gone through. I would not be who I am personally or as a leader without those challenges. My mother taught me what we call *Ubuntu*, a concept that encompasses the leadership qualities required for the 21st century. *Ubuntu* translates to: I am, because of you. Women have superpowers and it's time to unleash them! *Wathinta umfazi, wathinta imbokodo* is a Zulu saying: You strike a woman, you strike a rock. This is particularly so as women get to C-Suite positions in male-dominated workplaces. Let us all shine our lights and lead the way for others to shine theirs. This is how we rise and lift others to rise.

As I was finishing writing the first draft of my book, I received a call: '*Hi Dr. Patience Mpofu. We would like to inform you that you are the winner of the 2019 Pan African CEO Global Most Influential Woman in Mining in Africa award*'. I just said, '*Thank you. I AM ENOUGH*'. I have unleashed my superpowers!

* * *

As I drifted to sleep after finally submitting my manuscript for publishing, I could hear the tears of joy of a woman working in a male-dominated (STEM) workplace like mining, thinking to herself, *I too can unleash my superpowers*!

The End

Exercise

You can watch the video of Patience climbing a pole in Fiji and the inspirational interviews of 30 global women leaders in STEM here: www.unleashingmysuperpowers.com/bonuses.

REFERENCES

Achebe, Chinua. 1958. *Things Fall Apart.* Nigeria: William Heinemann.

Australia. https://en.wikipedia.org/wiki/Australia.

Banaji, M.R and Greenwald, A.G. 2013. *Blindspot: Hidden Biases of good people.* New York, Delacorte Press

Beckton, Clare, and Umut Riza Okzan. 2012. *The Pathway Forward: Creating Gender Inclusive Leadership in Mining and Resources.* Report, Carleton University: Centre for Women in Politics and Public Leadership.

Bloomberg. 2021. Invest in more equal future. Bloomberg Gender Equality Index

Bohnet, Iris. 2016. *What Works: Gender Equality by Design.* Harvard University Press.

Brazil. https://en.wikipedia.org/wiki/Brazil.

Buolamwini, Joy, and Timnit Gebru. 2018. *Gender Shades: Intersectional Accuracy Disparities in Commercial Gender Classification.* MLR Press.

Byrne, Rhonda. 2006. *The Secret.* New York: Atria Books, Beyond Words Publishing, a division of Simon & Schuster.

Catalyst: 2021. *http://catalyst.org/research/women-ceos-of-the-sp-500*
Chamorro-Premuzic, Tomas, Rosabeth Moss Kanter, Amy Jen Su, and Peter Bregman. 2019. *Confidence (HBR Emotional Intelligence Series).* Harvard Business Review Press.

Chen, Serena. 2018. *Give Yourself a Break: The Power of Self-Compassion.* Harvard Business Review, September 1.

Chile. https://en.wikipedia.org/wiki/Chile.

Corkindale, Gill. 2008. *Overcoming Imposter Syndrome.* Harvard Business Review, May 7.

Cuddy, Amy. 2012. *Your body language may shape who you are.* TED.com. June.

https://www.ted.com/talks/amy_cuddy_your_body_language_may_shape_who_you_are.

Doidge, Norman. 2007. *The Brain that Changes Itself.* London: Viking Press, Penguin Random House.

Dodds, Glen Lyndon. 1998. The Zulus and Matabele: Warrior Nations. Arms and Armour. ISBN 978-1-85409-381-3

Duckworth, Angela. 2017. *GRIT: Why Passion and Resilience are the Secret to Success.* London: Ebury Publishing, part of Penguin Randon House.

Fels. A. 2004. *The truth about how women become leaders.* Harvard Business Review.

Garcia, Hector, and Francesc Miralles. 2017. *IKIGAI: The Japanese Secret to a Long and Happy Life.* London: Penguin Random House.

Gilbert, Elizabeth. 2006. *Eat, Pray, Love*. United States: Penguin Random House

Helgesen, Sally, and Marshall Goldsmith. 2018. *How Women Rise*. New York: Anchor Books, a division of Random House Inc.

Hill, Napolean. 2014. *Think and Grow Rich*. London: Ebury Publishing, a Random House group company.

King, Michelle P, 2020. *The Fix: How to Overcome the Invisible Barriers That Are Holding Women Back at Work*. New York: Atria Books, a part of Simon & Schuster.

Kiyosaki, Robert. 1997. *Rich Dad Poor Dad*. Werner Book Ed.

Kohoe, John. 2001. *Mind Power into the 21st Century*. Zoetec Books. Lapin, David. 2020. *Blog: R&R*. Lapin International - September 09. https://lapininternational.com/leadership-blog/r-r/.

Mandivenga, EC. 1983. *Islam in Zimbabwe*. Gweru, Zimbabwe: Mambo Press.

Manuela. P. 2020. *Times up for toxic Workplaces*. Harvard Business Review

Mathiva, M.E.R. 1992. *The Basena/Vamwenye/Balemba*. Zimbabwe: Morester Printers.

McClean et al. 2021. *Stop making excuses for toxic leaders*. Harvard Business Review.

Hidden Figures. 2016. Movie. Directed by Theodore Melfi. https://en.wikipedia.org/wiki/Hidden_Figures.

Minerals Council of Australia. https://minerals.org.au.

Minerals Council of South Africa. https://www.mineralscouncil.org.za. Mourant, A, A Kopec, and K Domaniewska-Sobczak. 1978. *The Genetics of the Jews.* Oxford University Press.

Mullen, J.E. 1969. *The Arab Builders of Zimbabwe.* Rhodesia.

Nyrop, Richard F. 1985. *The Yemens: Country Studies.* Washington, DC: American University Foreign Area Studies.

Parfitt, T. 2000. *Journey to the Vanished City: The Search for a Lost Tribe of Israel.* New York: Vintage, a part of Penguin Random House. Porter, Michael, and Mark Kramer. 2011. *Creating Shared Value.* Harvard Business Review.

Risse, Leonora. 2020. 'That advice to women to 'lean in', be more confident… it doesn't help, and data show it' in *The Conversation - RMIT*, October 14.

Sandberg, Sheryl. 2013. *Lean In: Women, Work and the Will to Lead.* London: Penguin Random House.

Sharma, Robin. 2018. *The 5am Club.* London: HarperCollins Publications.

Smith, Emily, Esfahani. 2017. *The Power of Meaning: The True Route to Happiness.* London: Penguin Random House.

Spurdle, A, M Hammer, and T Jenkins. 1994. 'The Alu polymorphism in southern African populations and its relationship to other Y-specific polymorphisms' in *The American Journal of Human genetics*, 319-330. *The 2021 World's Best Cities list is out and these 5 Aussie cities made the cut.* Business Insider. November 11. https://www.businessinsider.com.au/best-cities-in-the-world-australia-2020-11

Tannen, D. 1995. *The power of talk: who gets heard and why*. Harvard Business Review

Thomas, Mark, T Parfitt, D Weiss, K Skorecki, J Wilson, M le Roux, N Bradman, and D Goldstein. 2000. 'Y Chromosomes Traveling South: The Cohen Modal Haplotype and the Origins of the Lemba—the "Black Jews of Southern Africa"' in *The American Journal of Human Genetics*, February: 674-686.

Travis, J. 2009. *The priests' chromosome? DNA analysis supports biblical story of the Jewish priesthood*. Science News, June 30: 218-219.

Victoria Falls: https://whc.unesco.org/en/list/509/

Wittenberg-Cox, Avivah. 2020. *What Do Countries With The Best Coronavirus Responses Have In Common? Women Leaders*. South Carolina: Forbes.

Woetzel, J. and Magdavhav A. 2015. *How advancing women's equality can add $12 trillion to global growth by 2025*. McKinsey Global Institute Report.

Made in the USA
Monee, IL
07 July 2026

56552152R00135